FIRST JOHN

a
Commentary

FIRST JOHN

a

Commentary

GORDON H. CLARK

THE TRINITY FOUNDATION
JEFFERSON, MARYLAND

ISBN: 0-940931-94-X

Contents

Books by Gordon H. Clark

Readings in Ethics (1931)
Selections from Hellenistic Philosophy (1940)
A History of Philosophy (coauthor, 1941)
A Christian Philosophy of Education (1946, 1988)
A Christian View of Men and Things (1952, 1991)
What Presbyterians Believe (1956)[1]
Thales to Dewey (1957, 1989)
Dewey (1960)
Religion, Reason and Revelation (1961, 1986)
William James (1963)
Karl Barth's Theological Method (1963)
The Philosophy of Science and Belief in God (1964, 1987)
What Do Presbyterians Believe? (1965, 1985)
Peter Speaks Today (1967)[2]
The Philosophy of Gordon H. Clark (1968)
Biblical Predestination (1969)[3]
Historiography: Secular and Religious (1971)
II Peter (1972)[2]
The Johannine Logos (1972, 1989)
Three Types of Religious Philosophy (1973, 1989)
First Corinthians (1975, 1991)
Colossians (1979, 1989)
Predestination in the Old Testament (1979)[3]
I and II Peter (1980)
Language and Theology (1980)
First John (1980, 1992)
God's Hammer: The Bible and Its Critics (1982, 1987)
Behaviorism and Christianity (1982)
Faith and Saving Faith (1983, 1990)
In Defense of Theology (1984)
The Pastoral Epistles (1984)
The Biblical Doctrine of Man (1984, 1992)
The Trinity (1985, 1990)
Logic (1985, 1988)
Ephesians (1985)
Clark Speaks From the Grave (1986)
Logical Criticisms of Textual Criticism (1986, 1990)
First and Second Thessalonians (1986)
Predestination (1987)
The Atonement (1987)
The Incarnation (1988)
Today's Evangelism: Counterfeit or Genuine? (1990)
Essays on Ethics and Politics (1992)
Sanctification (1992)

[1] Revised in 1965 as *What Do Presbyterians Believe?*
[2] Combined in 1980 as *I & II Peter*.
[3] Combined in 1987 as *Predestination*.

Foreword

The major themes of John's first letter are truth and love. Perhaps no other New Testament author spends as much time discussing those ideas as John does in his Gospel, Revelation, and three letters. The word *love* appears over one hundred times in John's five works; the words *true* and *truth* appear about 85 times. John obviously thought the two ideas were very important. He also thought they were closely connected. God is both truth and love. God is truth himself, and God acts in love: "In this is love, not that we loved God, but that he loved us and sent his Son to be the propitiation for our sins." Christians are to believe the truth and act in love. If one acts according to the truth, one is acting in love.

Modern churches disagree with both John's emphasis and his demonstration of the connection between truth and love. They think that truth has little or nothing to do with love; in fact, truth may actually be opposed to love. Modern thinking says: Love is a matter of the heart; truth is a matter of the head. Truth leads to arrogance and pride; love leads to service and humility. Truth is cold and intellectual; love is warm and spiritual.

One finds none of this sort of thinking in John. For example, John addresses his second letter to "the chosen lady and her children, whom I love in truth; and not only I, but also all who know the truth, for the sake of the truth which abides in us and will be with us forever." He ends his benediction in verse 3 with the words, "in truth and love." John continues to emphasize the close connection between love and truth in verses 9 and 10: "Anyone who goes too far and does not abide in the teaching of Christ, does not have God; the one who

5

abides in the teaching has both the Father and the Son. If any one come to you and does not bring this teaching, do not receive him into your house, and do not give him a greeting . . . ." John commands that no hospitality be shown to any teacher who does not teach the truth—no hospitality, not even a greeting. That is love. John explains why: "for the one who gives him a greeting participates in his evil deeds."

Modern thinking says John's command is unloving. But that merely means that the modern thinkers not only misunderstand what John means by *truth*, but also what he means by *love*. Indiscriminate, perhaps *promiscuous* would be an even better word, affection seems to be the modern meaning of love, but Christian love is something quite different. John says clearly what he means by love: "For this is the love of God, that we keep his commandments." "And this is love, that we walk according to his commandments." One can agree with the modern thinkers or one can agree with John; one can be either an unbeliever or one can be a Christian. What one cannot do, for it would be neither truthful nor loving, is to claim to be a Christian and to disagree with John.

In his commentary, Gordon Clark deals with John's themes of love and truth in great detail. This book is a verse-by-verse commentary on John's letter, and the detailed study will richly reward the attentive reader. John wrote his letter so that we might not sin. Let us study it thoroughly, believe the truth, and act in love.

John W. Robbins
March 1992

Preface

THE first, the most important, the indispensable, the sine qua non aim of a commentary is to explain the text. Otherwise it might be a book of some value for other purposes, but if it doesn't tell what the text means, it is not a good commentary.

Not all commentaries are good. John Cotton wrote a commentary on First John that explains the meaning only once in a while. George Hutcheson wrote a book on John's Gospel, 437 pages of double columns, which explained hardly a single verse. The Puritan commentaries are usually excellent in their theology, but even here they wander from the text in irrelevant profusion. Their applications of doctrine are naturally directed to the conditions of their own day, or if they consider more universally human failings they are often tedious and sometimes trifling. In any case many are not good commentaries because they do not explain what the text means. Difficult as well as easy verses are assumed to be equally clear.

Now, it is certainly appropriate to develop doctrine so far as the text allows; in fact, this is what explanation is. It is also appropriate to make applications. Indeed, one of the reasons for writing another commentary is to make applications to the conditions of a later century, conditions that did not exist two or three hundred years earlier. America today is not Puritan England. Yes, there are universally human failings; the biblical principles apply to all ages; but the situation is like the traffic laws. Collisions on the road were to be avoided under James and Charles, but we need laws now of which they never could have thought.

The overarching aim, the fundamental purpose, the permeating theme of the present commentary is the explanation of the text. A few easy verses may need little comment, especially if their preceding context has been made clear. More difficult passages have several more or less plausible interpretations. There are difficulties also which earlier commentators have either not seen, or if seen, have ignored. Some readers may wish that this commentary had ignored them. But honest dealing with the Word of God forbids. It is better to be honestly in doubt than blissfully mistaken. This commentary does not omit any difficulty for fear of embarrassment. Since the writer is not infallible, the reader is at liberty to disagree and reject; but the price of this liberty is to face the problem.

The difficulties, both major and minor, are of three types. First are those elements of Greek grammar necessary to make a good translation. Every translation is to some degree an interpretation; and in this commentary the degree is higher than in our printed Bibles. The reader should consider each verse carefully. Most of the readers, of course, will know little if any Greek. They need not, however, be dismayed. The words are written out in Latin letters, and anyone who has had a course in German knows that nouns have cases. Even in English the personal pronouns have cases. The reason for using Greek here and there is to show how translation is itself interpretation. Each instance is explained in the most elementary terms, and if anyone feels uncomfortable, it will more likely be a person who knows Greek rather than one who does not.

The second type of difficulty concerns Higher Criticism. In previous years it was the Old Testament that suffered most from attacks by Wellhausen and others. Now the New Testament has come within their range. Since the subject is extremely technical, this commentary does not spend much space on it. But one point seemed necessary: Bultmann needed to be demythologized.

The third type of difficulty, the most frequent, the most important, and basically the only one that really matters, is the theological. The Apostle John is telling us various things about God. In the very beginning he announces his subject as the Logos, the same Logos with which, with whom, he opens his Gospel. We want to understand what he says. This is theology. This is the study of which God is the object. John wants to tell us about God, and, I hope, we all want to know what he meant.

So, my good reader, read carefully.

The First Chapter

1:1. That which was from the beginning, that which we have heard, that which we have seen with our eyes, that which we contemplated, and our hands touched, namely the Word of life. . . .

BEFORE the commentary commences, and with reference to the Epistle as a whole, one may note that the Roman Catholic "Jerusalem Bible," both French and English, print the Epistle as poetry. Other translators and editors print small sections of various Epistles as poetry. Have these people ever read Homer or Sophocles? Have they ever heard of scansion? Let us rather understand and enjoy good prose.

The translation: "That which" is a neuter pronoun. Since the object, identified at the end of the verse, "the word of life," is grammatically masculine, the neuter pronoun seems strange. The reader is thus confronted with a difficulty right at the start, and it turns out to be more difficult than anyone at first reading could imagine. Does *logos* refer to Christ himself? That would make *logos* masculine not only in grammar, but in reality also. Or does *logos* mean the gospel as proclaimed? If so, the neuter "that which" is appropriate. Comment is called for.

First, let us state the difficulty more precisely. The words "from the beginning" remind us of John 1:1, and we are tempted to think of the pre-incarnate Son of God. But the disciples *heard* a message, and *saw* Jesus. Calvin saw the difficulty, though perhaps not so clearly as

9

contemporary factors force it upon us today. At any rate, Calvin considers an opponent who insinuates that the passage is nonsense because "the evidence of the senses little availed the present subject, for the power of Christ cannot be perceived by the eyes." Calvin does not reply with a defense of sensation, but rather refers to John's Gospel 1:14, "We have seen his glory." For, says Calvin, "he was not known as the Son of God by the external form of his body, but because he gave illustrious proofs of his Divine power. . . ." Calvin does not instanciate these proofs, but he clearly rejects the idea that "seeing with the eyes" is literal sensation.

He then adds that the last phrase of the verse, "the Word is life," is properly rephrased as "the living word" because it is the Word that gives life.

To investigate this difficulty and to try to discover precisely what John meant, one must meticulously examine each phrase. The Christian will find the subject of great importance and well worth the time and trouble it takes.

Perhaps the easiest way to begin is by attending to the verbs *contemplated* and *touched*. These two verbs have both a physical and a nonphysical meaning. The first, "beheld," could be an exact synonym for "we have seen with our eyes" literally understood. But it also means intellectual contemplation. The second, "touched," can refer to a literal touching with the fingers, and it can also mean to test or examine.

Next comes the English word *namely,* the Greek preposition *peri,* translated *of* in the King James version. *Peri* with the genitive often denotes the object of the verb, which is here "the Word of life." *Namely* seems to make the sense a bit clearer than the preposition *of:* We have contemplated, regarded, looked at, and touched the Word of life.

A great many people take this verse in its strictest literal meaning. The disciples saw Jesus with their eyes, as anyone may see a house or an apple tree. With their ears they heard sounds, just as we today hear the sounds of someone talking across the fence or the static on the radio. The disciples touched Jesus with their hands, probably embraced him as the Middle Eastern custom still is. To say otherwise is to deny the incarnation; and anyone who denies that Jesus came in the flesh is of the antichrist, as John himself will say in 4:2-3.

Yet, one must always bear in mind that a thought plainly stated in one verse is not necessarily to be found in another. There can be no doubt that John opposes *Docetism,* the view that Christ was a sort of phantom or ghost. In the following century the Gnostics, for certain peculiar reasons that need not be explained here, held some such view. But it clearly contradicts John and all the New Testament. Nevertheless, what this first verse means must be determined on the basis of its own wording, and the wording must be compared with identical or similar wording throughout the Bible.

Even the commentators, or some of them, who hold that the object referred to here is Jesus in the flesh, see something else here also. Note that the verb *see* in this last sentence is not a literal seeing with the eyes. But, you say, does not John say explicitly, "we have seen with our eyes"? He surely did. No one can deny it. But at the very least, many commentators see more.

A. W. Pink, a widely known commentator, and among strict evangelicals well esteemed, published a book on First John in 1865 or thereabouts. After stating that the purpose of the Epistle "is to place all to whom [the Epistle] comes in the same advantageous position which he himself and his fellow-apostles enjoyed," he continues:

> When he says, "That which we have seen and heard, declare we unto you," I cannot doubt that he means to indicate generally the *"apostles' doctrine"* (Acts 2:42)—the common doctrine of all of them alike. . . . We cannot make you as well as we ourselves have been, not at least as far as knowledge comes through the direct information of the senses. . . . We have had a personal acquaintance with Jesus in the flesh. . . . We cannot make you partakers with us in that way of *"knowing Christ after the flesh"* (II Cor. 5:16). . . . Even if we could, we would not consider that enough for you . . . for we have ourselves experienced a great change since the sensible means . . . of knowledge . . . have been withdrawn. The former knowledge of Christ . . . ranks with us among the *"old things that have passed away."* . . . *"Therefore from now on we know no man according to the flesh . . ."* (II Cor. 5:16).

Arthur Pink believed that the Bible is true throughout. Some commentators do not. These latter can be divided into three groups. First, there are those who allege minor errors in the Bible, while still accepting its major doctrines. Second are those who have discarded some of the fundamental doctrines. The writings of these men must be scrutinized with special care, for they profess a certain respect for

Scripture and try to reinterpret it so as to exclude the doctrines they dislike. That is, they have claimed, for example, that the Scripture itself does not teach the vicarious atonement. Then, third, and more recently the radical shift to the left often acknowledges that the orthodox interpretation is correct. The reason is that the Bible for them is mythology, and its message is not the grammatical interpretation of the text, but a demythologized theology that suits their taste. Hence, they can admit that the Scripture teaches a propitiatory sacrifice, but the true meaning is a psychiatric procedure to remove guilt feelings. For this reason one is more likely to find a good interpretation in the present day liberals than in the earlier modernist books. Even so, one wonders if the study of modern liberals is worth the time, for it is necessary to endure a great amount of existentialism to find a valuable thought.

Let us now consider another commentator on these puzzling verses. B. F. Westcott was a good scholar who can probably be classified with the first group. The following gives an incomplete notion of his views expressed in five columns of small print.

> *That which . . . handled . . .* brings into distinct prominence the different elements of the apostolic message. Of this, part extended [back] to the utmost limits of time, being absolutely when time began; part was gradually unfolded in the course of human history. . . . These truths were gradually realized in the course of ages. . . . The "hearing" "concerning the word of life" is not to be limited to the actual preaching of the Lord during his visible presence. . . . *Handled:* there can be no doubt that the exact word is used with a distinct reference to the invitation of the Lord after his resurrection: *Handle me* (Luke 24:39). . . . Hence the word of life is the whole message from God to man . . . the whole *Gospel.*

Thus Westcott understands the Word to be the gospel message, though he also includes the visible experiences of the disciples with the incarnate Jesus.

Westcott wrote in 1883; Robert Cameron wrote his commentary in 1899. Here are some of his ideas.

> Life in its essence can never be seen. . . . John is writing of the Life . . . that Life which is eternal . . . the Word of Life. A word is that which expresses the unseen thought. . . . The use of the term "Word" does not necessarily imply the spoken word.

This is not all that this author says; and some reader may think that

Dr. Cameron, by his other statements, almost denies the sentences here quoted. But still the quoted sentences are his.

Much more recently (1964) J. R. W. Stott had this to say:

> Two questions concerning the phrase *of the Word of life* need to be discussed. The first is whether *logos* is here personal or impersonal, whether it is the semi-technical designation of the Son found in the Prologue of the Fourth Gospel or whether it is rather a synonym for "the word of the gospel" (Acts 15:7).

In an additional note (pp. 66–67) Stott remarks that the Gospel uses the term *logos* four times in an absolute sense, that is, not Word of something, but simply Word; whereas the Epistle has "word of life," and that the Epistle's emphasis falls on *life* and not on *logos.* This note supports the conclusion (p. 58) "that the *Word of life* is not a title for the Son, the Word or *Logos* . . . but an expression for the gospel." At the end of the paragraph Stott adds, "In other words, what the apostle stresses in his proclamation of the gospel is the historical manifestation of the Eternal." This last sentence is not obviously consistent with the previous conclusion. The phrase "the historical manifestation of the Eternal" strikes one's mind as a designation of the incarnate Son, rather than as the gospel message. Perhaps Stott would say that the gospel message is itself an historical process. At any rate he said explicitly that "the Word of life is not a title for the Son." This receives corroboration on the next page (p. 59) where he distinctly says, "The Eternal Son was before his historical manifestation; the preaching of the gospel came after." Apparently then "the historical manifestation of the Eternal" is not the incarnate Jesus. Yet he seems to contradict himself and identify the Word with Jesus, when he continues, "This stress on the material manifestation of Christ to men's ears, eyes, and hands is of course directed primarily against the heretics who were troubling the Church" (p. 61) by denying the incarnation.

The present commentator now aims to show that the Epistle has little interest in the *material* and *sensory* manifestation of Christ, though this may seem paradoxical in view of the words eyes, ears, and hands.

Paradoxical or not, the text itself rather clearly indicates that John was not, certainly not primarily, concerned with visual and tactual sensations. Somewhat confusedly, the commentators just quoted say the same thing. More or less clearly denying that the *logos* is the Second Person of the Trinity, they interpret it to mean the gospel message. But the gospel message cannot literally be heard with the ears. Presumably Jesus spoke Aramaic. The disciples heard certain Aramaic sounds. John declares this message in Greek. The Greek sounds are totally different; but the message is identical. The sound *dabar* is not the sound *lalei* or *eipon*. *Memra*, if Jesus used it, is not pronounced *sophia*. We today use the sounds *word, speak, wisdom,* and these are neither the Greek nor the Hebrew sounds. The important factor is the intellectual content, not the auditory impressions. When John in verse three completes the sentence by saying, "these things we declare unto you," he is totally uninterested in the psychology of sensation.

But for this very reason, as well as for some others, we should not so sharply distinguish the gospel message from the incarnate Son and say either (1) that *logos* means the gospel and not the Son, or (2) that *logos* means the Son and not the gospel. To understand how they coincide requires some attention, and likely not everybody will be convinced.

First, one must ask, where is the *beginning?* In John 1:1 the beginning is in eternity. But if *logos* is identified with the proclamation, the beginning must be placed in Genesis 3, or in A.D. 30. The announcement of the message of salvation was first made to Adam and Eve. But if one stresses "what we have seen," the beginning was during Christ's earthly lifetime. If the beginning be identified as God's revelation to Adam, John could not possibly have been speaking of the incarnate Jesus. But perhaps this beginning seems implausible to most Christians. The choice then remains between eternity and A.D. 30. True, the Epistle does not stress creation as the Gospel does; but thoughts can be included in a paragraph without being stressed later on. It is surely possible, if not preferable, to think that John has the eternal Son in mind. Naturally, the Second Person of the Trinity can no more be seen with the eyes, literally taken, than the message of the gospel can. The eternal Logos had neither visible color nor extension in space.

But someone is sure to ask, If John was thinking about eternity past, how could he have mentioned his own eyes and hands? This is a good point. Further, he who asks the question may continue and say, the reference to sight and hearing definitely indicates the visual and tactual sensations of John himself. This is not such a good point. John was a Jew, of a priestly family (one may infer); and like Paul he knew the Old Testament thoroughly. Now, Hebrew mentality, which God used to proclaim his message, was strongly metaphorical. All languages make use of metaphor. The English of England is replete with similies and analogies:

> Time, like an ever-rolling stream,
> Bears all its sons away;
> They fly forgotten as a dream
> Dies at the opening day.

The two main metaphors of flowing and flying are literarily pleasing, but no one thinks of taking them seriously.

General reflections on metaphorical language, however, do not constitute the main argument. Following are some phrases from the Old Testament, which form the background of John's expressions. Everyone of them uses a sense organ as a metaphor, and some use John's double expression of *seeing* with the *eyes*.

Proverbs 3:7	Be not wise in thine own eyes.
Isaiah 6:10	Shut their eyes, lest they see with their eyes and hear with their ears, and understand with their heart.
Isaiah 11:3	He shall not judge after the sight of his eyes, nor reprove after the hearing of his ears.
Isaiah 44:18	He hath shut their eyes that they cannot see.
Jeremiah 5:21	. . . which have eyes and see not; which have ears and hear not.
Ezekiel 12:2	. . . which have eyes and see not; which have ears and hear not.
Ezekiel 40:4	Behold with thine eyes and hear with thine ears.

Then in the New Testament:

Matthew 13:14–16	By hearing ye shall hear and shall not understand, and seeing ye shall see and shall not perceive. . . . Their eyes they have closed, lest at any time they should see with their eyes and hear with their ears, and should understand with their heart. . . . But blessed are your eyes, for they see, and your ears, for they hear.

Someone might now wish to make a last ditch stand in defending sensation and empirical theology. Would John, he might ask, have used the words of Isaiah? If he says, "see with the eyes," would he not have meant what he said? The answer is clear: John not only might have used Isaiah's metaphors, he did. He explicitly quoted Isaiah.

John 12:40   He hath blinded their eyes and hardened their hearts, that
                    they should not see with their eyes. . . .

It will be "seen" that in none of these verses does seeing refer to sensory perception, even when the phrase is emphasized by the addition of "with our eyes." There are other verses, too. Exodus 15:14, "people shall hear and be afraid," and the following two verses speak—does anyone hear the sound?—of a fear that mere auditory impressions could not produce. In Numbers 9:8 did God produce air vibrations that set Moses' ear-drums in vibration? There is no denying that God could have done so; the question is, did he do so? The hearing in Deuteronomy 1:43 is not sensation, but obedience. Even more definite is

Deuteronomy 29:4 Yet the Lord hath not given you an heart to perceive, and
                  eyes to see, and ears to hear, unto this day.

Of course, the Israelites had been born with and still possessed eyes and ears. But the eyes and ears of the verse were not sense organs. It should be clear that in such verses no physico-chemical processes are meant (cf. II Kings 14:11 and Job 27:9). Furthermore, when it is said that God hears our prayers, or that his eyes go to and fro over the earth, it cannot escape notice that God, who is a pure incorporeal Spirit, has no sense organs.

There are many other such verses; and if this small number has seemed tedious, or if someone fails to understand why so much space is thus wasted, the answer is that many people in the pews take I John 1:1 literally, as do some commentators. John Cotton (1657?) defines the object of verse one as "Christ Jesus in himself [and] as man, as being heard, seen, and grasped by the senses." Some theologians also try to use the passage in defense of an empirical system of apologetics. Hence there is need of more than enough references in order to rebut empirical contentions.

To summarize: neither the Logos, the Son of God, nor the gospel message is a sensory object. But to anticipate: Is the object "seen" the incarnate Jesus or the message he preached? Could it possibly be both? If so, how?

The note appended to the translation pointed out the peculiarity of the neuter relative pronoun. Of course, if *logos* is the message, the neuter is appropriate; but if the *logos* is the person, it is perplexing. John Cotton, in spite of his acceptance of sensory experience, makes an ingenious, a fundamentally good, but as expressed a too highly imaginative, suggestion. "There was something of the word of life which was from the beginning, namely, his Godhead. And again there was something in the same word of life that was seen and heard, namely, his manhood. If there is something both eternal and approachable by the senses," the neuter includes both better than the masculine could. Lenski's view is similar, but more reasonable and less imaginative: "The neuter conveys more than the masculine would, namely in the addition to the person all that this person was and is and ever will be for us" (p. 370). On the whole this seems to be correct; but possibly it can be shown how the message and the person are one. Most commentators do not undertake to explain this unity. Westcott, from whom we might expect careful grammatical analysis, says simply that the neuter "can have no direct personal reference." But if a relative pronoun, or demonstrative, refers to a combination, the message and the person, a neuter is quite permissible. Indeed, a masculine would be highly suspicious. The conclusion, therefore, is that the neuter refers to a combination, though how the two factors are combined is not explained in the text.

Something has already been said about the *beginning*. Those who identify the *Word* with the message must date the beginning either with Adam and Eve, or with the first apostolic preaching. If, however, it is possible to interpret the phrase in accordance with the first verse of the Gospel without producing any impossible conflict, it would seem better to do so. Furthermore, in verse two, the verb *was made evident*, or *was manifested*, plausibly presupposes a previous condition in which *the Word* was not evident. One must decide whether or not this expression better fits the Son of God himself than it does the message. Can anyone positively deny that this manifestation was the incarnation? I find this much more plausible than the beginning of a manifest proclamation to Adam.

The next phrases have already been discussed. To the present writer they cannot possibly mean sensory experience, much less imply an empirical apologetics.

The last phrase in verse one is "the Word of life." This phrase can without question mean a message preached. In the Gospel (6:68) John records Peter as using the phrase "the words of eternal life." Granted, Peter said *rhēmata*, and not *logous*. But the next footnote will minimize the difference. Calvin and Cotton took the phrase in the Epistle to mean the message, but both connected it somehow with the person. Westcott, however, is so anxious to rule out the person and emphasize the preaching that he goes rather too far. He asserts that the emphasis in verse 1 falls on *life* and not on *logos*. Not the *word* of life, but the word of *life*. It is the *life* and not the *word* which is said to have been manifested. To most of us this seems a bit queer. We would probably think that *life* was more personal than *word*. But Westcott is obsessed with the Logos of the Gospel, who is clearly a person. Now, it is true that the next verse says that the *life* was manifested. But it also says that something must be "announced" or "declared." Life, strictly speaking, cannot be declared or preached. A message can. This by itself ought to please Westcott. Where he goes wrong, in the opinion of the present writer, is his sharp distinction between the personal Word and the spoken or written word. At any rate, the apostles preached the word, message, written word, or doctrine of life. It was the doctrine which produced the life. Note, too, that the Greek word *logos* can mean *doctrine* as well as a *word*. It can mean a book, and a mathematical ratio as well.[1]

Westcott also says, and it is unfortunate that he did not press it, "In a most true sense Christ is the gospel." Had he done so, the unity of the person and the message, which so many people mistakenly try to separate sharply, could have been clarified. Let us first ask, What is a human person? Is he arms and legs? Hardly, for they may be amputated without annihilating the person or changing him into another person. The Bible itself shows that Moses as a person could still discuss the doctrine of the atonement 13 or 14 centuries after his body had crumbled to dust. Both Christ and the thief were in paradise Friday night, though their bodies had been buried before sunset. A person is his mind. A person is his thoughts. The Apostle Paul said, "We have the mind of Christ." Paul had the mind of Christ (in part) because he understood the atonement in I Corinthians 1, and the wisdom of God in chapter 2. Christ, too, is his mind, of which the

---

[1]Compare my *Johannine Logos* (Jefferson, Maryland: The Trinity Foundation, 1989 [1972]) in which the identity of *logos* and *rhēma* is argued.

gospel message is a part. God is a spirit, an intelligence, a mind; God is truth, and the message is a part of that truth. Therefore the proclamation of the gospel is the proclamation of Christ. As Westcott said, though perhaps more than he meant, "In a most true sense Christ is the gospel."

It was said above that sometimes the most anti-Christian theologians do good exegesis. They can see the meaning because they do not have to believe it. Here Bultmann says, "Is not the meaning of *Logos* as a divine person also echoed in the term *logos?*"

In all this there is a profound philosophical problem that presumably has no place in a commentary. Yet the readers, or some of them, should be aware of it. The problem is, as has been said, the nature of the mind. John Locke in one way and Immanuel Kant in another made the mind "a something I know not what," or a "transcendental unity of apperception," equally unknowable. Hume reduced the person to a series of disconnected images. His empiricism required the sensory images and it also made a connection among them impossible. Those who find such problems challenging are cordially urged to attack them with vigor. Here the commentary can only assert, somewhat dogmatically, that the message and the person cannot be separated. If we both understand, as Bultmann seems to, and also believe, as Bultmann surely does not, that is, understand and believe the doctrine, we like Paul and John have the mind of Christ, namely Christ himself.

Some of the exegesis just given has received support from the following verse or verses. The meaning of a verse can rarely, and never completely, be determined within the verse itself. Even such a simple historical statement, such as "David was king of Israel," requires for a larger understanding some knowledge of Israel. In doctrinal matters dependence on other verses is still more obvious. Hence it is time to proceed to verse 2.

1:2.   And the life was made manifest, and we have seen and we testify and we announce [or, preach] to you this eternal life which was with the Father and which was made manifest to us.

The translation: There are no particular difficulties with the translation. It would be hard to find a simpler sentence in all Greek literature. Well, a simple historical statement in Xenophon's *Anabasis* might possibly be as simple. We proceed then to the interpretation.

One thing that makes the verse so simple is that it is parenthetical. The main sentence begins in verse 1, skips verse 2, and continues through verse 3. Grammatically verse 2 stands alone.

Some people of mystical and pietistic bent wish to divorce the life from the Logos. Has not nearly everyone heard the silly cliche, "Life is deeper than logic"? Do not chapel speakers in evangelical colleges warn the students not to study too much on the ground that we are interested in a *person* and not a theology? Why don't they try to persuade the students to drop out? That would be much more pious, wouldn't it? But John, particularly in his Gospel, makes such a view impossible: "the words which I have spoken to you are spirit and are life." Here the Greek word for *words* is *rhēmata*, not *logoi;* and certainly not *logos.* Hence there is no possibility of identifying the life with the person of Christ as distinct from his words. Pietistic, mystical, neo-orthodox, nondoctrinal Christianity is simply not Christianity at all. Note that Christ very plainly said, "If anyone holds my doctrine, he shall not see death, ever." It is this doctrine, these words, or, more accurately the thoughts symbolized by the words, which John proclaims or announces. "This is life eternal, that they should know thee, the only true God and him whom thou hast sent, Jesus Christ." God is truth and is to be *known.*

The verse now adds, "which was with the Father." Whether he said it earlier or later, in the Gospel John uses the same preposition: "with God." This is at least a hint that the subject in the opening lines of the Epistle includes the pre-incarnate Son: it is neither the incarnate Son as such, nor the message somehow distinguished from the person, nor the person somehow distinguished from the contents of his mind.

This phrase, "with God" shows that the eternal life mentioned here is not the regenerated condition of John's addressees. In other places the apostle does indeed speak of the eternal life of those who believe the message. But here eternal life is that eternal life which was with, before, in the presence of, the Father. Hence the conclusion is further enforced that the object in view is the pre-incarnate Son of God. For this reason the verse also contributes something to the doctrine of the Trinity, but since the information is so meagre—simply that the Son is in the Father's presence—it will be inappropriate at this point to discuss the Trinity. One cannot, however, refrain from pointing out the parallel in the Gospel (1:18), "No one has ever seen [!] God; the only God [the only begotten God, the only begotten Son], who is in the bosom of the Father, this one explained [him]." These considerations also enforce what was said about the *beginning* in verse 1. It cannot be the incarnation, as Bultmann thinks, for what was made evident had not been previously evident, but had been in the presence of the Father.

This is the end of verse 2. It is a parenthesis which lengthens the sentence composing verses 1-3. Any thought that it is a scribal insertion is nonsense. The New Testament authors, as well as any authors, use parentheses. Their occurrence is no cause for suspicion. If some manuscript had omitted the verse, we might suspect an insertion, but apparently there is not a single one without it.

> **1:3.   What we have seen and heard, we proclaim also to you, in order that you also may have fellowship with us. And this our fellowship is with the Father and with his Son Jesus Christ.**

Since the parenthesis was about three lines long, the author recapitulates verse one in order to continue: "What we have seen and heard, we announce. . . ." John Cotton very stupidly insists, "The apostles taught nothing but what was manifest to the senses." When Peter confessed, "Thou art the Christ," Jesus replied, in effect, You never deduced that from sensory experience; that was a direct revelation from the Father. Can the Trinity be sensed? What color is justification, and how much does faith weigh? Is perseverance salt or sour? Is assurance, of which this Epistle has something to say, B flat or F sharp? Many good Christians who regularly sit in the pews Sunday after Sunday may think that the present diatribe against sensation, even if fairly obvious, is strange and overdone. It will not, however, seem strange to those who realize how many theologians try to base their apologetic system on sensory experience. Admittedly the diatribe is, though it ought not to have had to be, overdone.

When John says, *we* have seen and *we* proclaim, he probably is not using the editorial *we*. Presumably he has in mind all the apostles and many of the disciples. What is more puzzling is the word *you.* To whom is John preaching his message? As nearly all commentaries point out, the Epistle is not explicitly addressed to anybody. One is at liberty to suggest he meant it for the seven churches of his Apocalypse. But it is hard to believe that even Romans was meant for the city of Rome only. The apostles clearly recognized their worldwide mission. They knew they were writing for future generations in far off lands. No doubt when he says, ". . . that you also may have fellowship with us," he is thinking of some local group or groups; but even here the word *also* hints at others. Paul thought of Rome and of the world. There is no incompatibility between these two references.

The word *fellowship* merits some explanation. *Koinōnia* is the state of two persons who have something in common. Joint tenancy is a *koinōnia.* There is a *koinōnia* between two people who enjoy playing chess. Any common possession is a *koinōnia.* Here John wants to produce and maintain a common belief in the truths of Christianity. He proclaims information that will give believers something in common. Later in the Epistle there will be reflections on some persons who do not believe these common doctrines. Some in the visible church do not believe that the Logos came in the flesh. They entertain a false doctrine of the incarnation. Therefore they should be expelled from the communion, unless they voluntarily withdraw.

A. W. Pink makes a valuable comment at this point:

> That it implies intelligence and insight I need scarcely repeat; such intelligence and insight as the Spirit alone can give. No man naturally has it. [The fact that only the Spirit can produce belief does not make the doctrine believed any the less intelligible, intellectual, cognizable.] You may tell me, in my natural state, of tangible benefits of some sort coming to me through some arrangement between the Father and the Son. . . . The notion of my being let off from suffering the pains of hell . . . is a notion intelligible enough, congenial and welcome enough to my natural mind. But this is very different from my having fellowship in that matter. . . . I may be profoundly and most stupidly indifferent as to what that transaction really is, and what the Father and the Son are to one another in it. (pp. 4, 5)

Not only are the doctrines, for example, the propitiatory sacrifice of the next chapter, held in common by the addressees and the apostle; they are held in common by these and the Father and Son. To have fellowship with God is to believe his truth. God and man have fellowship when they think alike. Some of these thoughts are described in the remainder of the Epistle.

Doubtless there are many misunderstandings of the nature of fellowship. One of them, at least, has troubled Christendom for centuries. It infects several ecclesiastical bodies, and now and then breaks out in other churches not historically attached to it. The Greek Orthodox church makes salvation depend on fellowship with the Greek Orthodox church. It makes no difference what a person believes: official membership is essential. Rome said that outside the church there is no salvation; and to prove it they massacred thousands of Albigenses and Huguenots. Bultmann quotes Holtzmann and the Venerable Bede as follows: "There is fellowship with . . . the Father and the Son only by . . . virtue of the legitimate tradition. Holtzmann, 240, appropriately quotes Bede's comment on this point: 'For whoever desires to have fellowship with God ought first to be joined to the fellowship of the church.' "

But this is backwards and destructive of pure Christianity. Membership in a visible organization, even if it be a true church, does not come first. The first step in fellowship with the Father and the Son is belief in God's message. It is the doctrine that is of first importance. Second comes membership in some relatively pure church. Tradition is not even last. A visible church that makes tradition a basis for belief is not a true church at all, but, as the Westminster Confession says, a synagogue of Satan. Nothing, absolutely nothing, excuses disbelief in the doctrine. What we have in common with the Father and with the Son is the gospel, the message, the theology that the apostle is about to sample in the following verses. These are the things that constitute fellowship and produce joy.

1:4.   And these things we write in order that our joy may be full.

The translation: There is considerable manuscript evidence for reading the verse as, "We write these things to you that your joy may be full." The difference is insignificant for the meaning. The basis for choice is somewhat subjective. One argument is that a scribe might inadvertently change the unexpected *our* to the obvious *your*, rather than the reverse. Not only does *your* better fit the immediate context, but a scribe might well remember John 15:11, 16:24, and 17:13. The reading *our*, however, is intelligible on the assumption that the apostle's joy would not be complete unless his addressees had the same joy, too. So far as understanding the Epistle is concerned, the difference is insignificant.

The word *chara* means joy. There is no doubt about the translation. But it must be noted that in the Gospel Christ expresses his joy on a most unjoyous occasion. The three references just mentioned all occurred the night in which he was betrayed. He was facing the scourging and degradation by the soldiers, and the crucifixion the next morning. Joy? It was a joy rather different from what the word means in ordinary situations. Instead of the thoughtless emotions of party-goers, Christ's joy was a profound satisfaction. It was no superficial exuberance, but a solid conviction that he would now accomplish his aim. He saw the travail of his soul and was satisfied. This, too, must be the joy of the apostles and of those to whom he writes. Not that our sacrifices, whatever they may be, propitiate the Father, as Christ's did; but that we understand and are convinced of the completeness and efficacy of his sacrifices. This is a joy that transcends bubbling frothy emotions.

Here ends the introduction. However the Epistle may be outlined, these four verses are clearly the first unit. Some outlines of the remainder are better than others. A relatively poor outline simply lists the prominent idea in each paragraph. For example:

1:5–10	God Is Light
2:1–6	Christ Our Advocate
2:7–17	The New Commandment
2:18–27	The Antichrist
2:28–3:10	Children of God
3:11–18	Love One Another
3:19–24	Confidence before God
4:1–6	The Spirit of God and the Spirit of Antichrist
4:7–21	God Is Love
5:1–5	Faith Is the Victory over the World
5:6–12	The Witness concerning the Son
5:13–21	The Knowledge of Eternal Life

Such an outline is illogical and messy. It is a mere mention of some of the topics discussed. A much better outline was made by Plummer and somewhat modified by Alexander Ross. Its reproduction here shortens some lengthy headings. After the Preface it goes as follows:

I. God is Light   1:5-2:29
   A. Walking in the Light—Positive
      1. Fellowship with God   1:5-7
      2. Consciousness of sin   1:8-2:2
      3. Walking as Christ walked   2:3-6
      4. Love of the brethren   2:7-11
   B. Walking in the Light—Negative
      1. John's reason for writing   2:12-14
      2. The world and its ways   2:15-17
      3. The antichrists   2:18-26
      4. Avoid all these by abiding in Christ   2:27-29
II. God is Love   3:1-5:12
   A. Evidence of Sonship   3:1-24
      1. Present and future condition of the children of God   3:1-3
      2. Children of God and children of the devil   3:4-12
      3. Love and hate   3:13-24
   B. The Source of Sonship   4:1-5:20
      1. The Spirit of Truth and the Spirit of Error   4:1-6
      2. Love, the mark of the children of God   4:7-21
      3. Love makes Christ's yoke easy   5:1-5
      4. Threefold testimony to the incarnation   5:6-8
      5. Acceptance insures eternal life   5:9-12
   [The last nine verses]
      1. Intercessory prayer   5:13-17
      2. Three great Christian certainties   5:18-20
      3. A final warning   5:21

The reader will note that the subdivisions are not logical; and even discarding logic, Plummer could not fit in the last nine verses.

Perhaps the next outline will prove better. Again, after the Preface or Introduction it is as follows:

I. Fellowship with the Father   1:5-2:28
   (tested by righteousness, love, and belief)
   A. The Condition of Righteousness   1:5-2:6
      1. Confession of sin   1:5-2:2
      2. Actual obedience   2:3-6
   B. The Condition of Love   2:7-17
      1. Love is light   2:7-11
      2. Parenthesis   2:12-14
      3. Love of God excludes love of the world   2:15-17
   C. The Condition of Belief   2:18-28
      1. Heresy destroys fellowship   2:18-22
      2. Exhortation   2:23-28
II. Our Sonship (tested by righteousness, love and belief)   2:29-4:6
   A. Sonship Tested by Righteousness   2:29-3:10a
      1. Righteousness, a sign of sonship   2:29
      2. Sonship causes righteousness   3:1-7
      3. Sin is of the Devil   3:8-10a
   B. Sonship Tested by Love   3:10b-23
      1. Love, a sign to ourselves and to others   3:10b-15
      2. Christ's sacrifice, our example   3:16-18
      3. Love gives confidence   3:18-23
   C. Sonship Tested by Belief   3:23-4:6
      1. Belief in Christ is as much a commandment as love
         3:23-24
      2. The test of all spirits is the doctrine of the incarnation
         4:1-6
III. Closer Correlation of Righteousness, Love, and Belief   4:7-5:21
   A. Love and Belief   4:7-5:3
      1. God is Love   4:7-12
      2. Love demands belief   4:13-16
      3. Belief makes us sons and we must love God's other
         children 4:17-5:3a
   B. Righteousness and Belief   5:3b-21
      1. The believer overcomes the world   5:3b-5
      2. This depends on a true incarnation   5:6-13
      3. Belief gives assurance in prayer   5:14-20
Conclusion: Jesus Christ is the true God   5:21

No claim is made that this outline is faultless. Complaints about its inadequacy will occur at several points. Nevertheless, its general agreement with the text can be clearly seen. What is more, its evident logic, the subordination of lesser matters to greater, and the coordination of the main themes, recommends it over disjointed lists of apparently unrelated ideas. The outline could have included some still lower subpoints, but these will be considered in the commentary.

I. Fellowship with the Father
   A. The Condition of Righteousness

1:5. And this is the message which we have heard from him and announce to you, that God is light and there is no darkness in him whatsoever.

It is almost tautological to say that what God is determines the conditions of fellowship. Naturally, if we have something in common with God, God had it before we were born. Or, better, God was it. Among the many things God may be said to be, John chooses to say God is light. This important piece of theology is the message "we have heard from him." The last *him* mentioned in the introduction was "his Son Jesus Christ." The fact that these precise words are not reported in the Gospel as one of Jesus' sayings does not militate against the ascription here. If not these words, at least statements about Jesus as the light occur in John 1:4 (here connected with *life*), in 8:12, 11:9-10, 12:46, and elsewhere.

The question now is, What is meant by the term *light?* If omnipotence or omniscience are predicated of God, most people think they understand. But metaphorical language is always baffling. Remember how even the disciples, not to mention the multitudes, failed to understand Jesus' parables. The difficulty with figures of speech is that the figurative object has many qualities and it is usually difficult to determine what constitutes the likeness. To use an extreme but immediately applicable example, light travels at a velocity of 186,000 miles a second; but God doesn't take eight minutes to reach earth from the sun. Light through a prism produces a rainbow; but God is neither red nor blue. Of course, these are ridiculous examples; but they show that there are many qualities in the symbol, from which we must pick one. Often it is difficult to know which to pick. Indeed in this instance of light, it is hard to see anything to pick. Consider for a moment some other biblical metaphors. Isaiah 7:2 says Syria's heart was moved as the trees of the wood are moved with the wind. Here it is clear that a Syrian king's mind was changed in some way; but the analogy of trees in the wind does not explain how. In other passages the literal part of the comparison is missing and the difficulty worse. Sixteen verses later Isaiah says the Lord shall hiss for the fly in a distant river. What in the world does that mean? One of the most extreme examples is the vision of colors, animals, wings, and wheels in Ezekiel. Some metaphors, however, are not so wholly left unexplained, and other scriptural passages can give us some "light" on the statement "God is light."

The last sentence shows that the figure of *light* is common in ordinary English. But this very familiarity may itself cause confusion, since the figure seems to mean a number of things. Even in philosophy, as distinct from everyday language, light is a common figure, with different meanings. For Heraclitus and the Stoics the substance of the world was light, or at least fire. The emanation theory of Plotinus is based on or explained by a point center of light, the rays from which diminish in intensity as they recede. Aside from pagan Greek philosophy, Gnosticism in the second century, a religious movement that borrowed several Christian terms (e.g., truth, life, church, wisdom, Christ), also spoke of light. But are we to suppose that the Bible uses the metaphor in the same sense?

To pierce, if possible, the biblical symbolism, one must study the Bible. First, the Old Testament: Psalm 4:6 says, "Lord, lift thou up the light of thy countenance upon us." Here light symbolizes any one of a number of God's favors. Peace, sleep, and safety are mentioned in the context. Psalm 27:1 is the well-known verse, "The Lord is my light and my salvation." Safety from enemies is chiefly in mind. Psalm 36:9 is, "In thy light shall we see light." St. Augustine used this verse to teach that God is the source of all knowledge. This may not be very clear in the immediate context; but possibly other passages will support Augustine's interpretation. Such support soon appears. Psalm 43:3 is, "O send out thy light and thy truth, let them lead me." No one can rationally maintain that the word *and* connects two different thoughts here. The nouns *light* and *truth* are in apposition.

The term *truth* explains what the term *light* means. Not all verses are so clear. Psalm 97:11 says, "Light is sown for the righteous." The meaning is obscure, but at least we can say that light and righteousness are related; but if related, they are not identical. Then there is the "comfortable saying" of Isaiah 9:2, "The people that walked in darkness have seen a great light." It seems to indicate their rescue from death. But the context does not identify what the light is. The same prophet (60:1) also says, "Arise, shine, for thy light is come." An alternate reading is "Arise, be enlightened." This is contrasted with the darkness of the people. Yet out of this darkness the "Gentiles shall come to thy light." This begins to look as if the light is the light of truth, the light of the gospel; and the darkness is paganism. It does not precisely say that God is light. Yet this may be the meaning, for in verse 19 he adds, "the Lord shall be unto thee an everlasting light," which words are also repeated in the following verse.

Psalm 19:8 does not use the word *light* itself, but it says that the commandments of God enlighten the eyes. Obviously the word *eyes* is a symbol for *mind* and *understanding*. See also 119:105, 130. In this last verse, *words* give light. Proverbs 6:23 says, "the law is light." *Light*, therefore, is a figure of speech that means *information* from God. The information, necessarily, is a part[2] of God's mind. So much, then, for the Old Testament.

Some verses from the New Testament have already been mentioned. The life that was in Jesus was the light of men; this light enlightens every man that comes into the world. Some commentators strain the grammatical construction and order of words to make it say, this light coming into the world enlightens every man. But first, note that this interpretation cannot get rid of "every man." Second, if Christ enlightens every man, including Cain as well as Abel, the reference cannot be to Christ's incarnation. The enlightenment was operative throughout the Old Testament. Hence, the interpretation is to be

---

[2]The term *part* must be used, even though God is "without parts and passions." The reason is that the God of Abraham, Isaac, and Jacob, and the Father of our Lord and Savior Jesus Christ, is not a simple unity as Plotinus' One was—superior to the Divine Mind. We speak of the decrees of God, though the eternal decree is one. But it is a complex unity. We speak of three Persons, but of one God. Hence, if God knows that Abraham lived after Noah, and that Paul journeyed to Rome, we may and must speak of different truths or propositions in God's mind. The unity of the propositions consists in their being a single system.

rejected. St. Augustine uses this verse to base all knowledge, even the knowledge that the reprobate have, on Christ. And the theme is clearer here than in Isaiah. The reading of Augustine's *De Magistro*, especially the second half, is a requirement for the course.

Admittedly, the knowledge of the reprobate does not do them much good. Theirs "is the condemnation that light is come into the world, and men loved darkness rather than light." Once again, this *coming* is not the incarnation because the condemnation applies also to the antedeluvians. Perhaps we should not skip over John 8:12 and 12:35, 36, but some space must be reserved for the Epistles. II Corinthians 4:4 is a most important verse: "if our gospel be hid, it is hid to them that are lost, in whom the god of this world hath blinded the minds [*noēmata* = thoughts] of them which believe not, lest the light of the glorious gospel of Christ, who is the image of God, should shine unto them." Let it be emphasized: the light is the gospel, the good news, a certain amount of information to be understood. The god of this world gives his slaves false thoughts—*noēmata*—whereas the good news of Christ is true. This message, as the next verse says, is something to be preached. And the following verse uses the words, "the light of the knowledge [*gnōsis*] of God." Now we can return to First John and see that the light is the message he will preach in the Epistle. God is light because he is truth. The message is a part of the very mind of God himself. And in him is no error or falsehood at all.

John Cotton helps to make this clear:

> Light . . . is put for knowledge (Matt. 4:16; Eccl. 2:13). Hence ministers having knowledge are called lights (Matt. 5:14; Rom. 2:19). . . . Your light is your doctrine and holy life. . . . God . . . is said to be light because he makes us so; men of knowledge, scattering the darkness of ignorance (Psa. 91:10). . . . Hence at our first creation, God's image consisted in knowledge (Col. 3:10) and holiness (Eph. 4:24). . . . God is essentially knowledge, and so his holiness is himself. (p. 35)[3]

---

[3]If any reader think that these remarks on metaphor go too far, denigrate literary beauty, and serve up the dry, unpalatable bones of literal statement, the reply need not depend on refuting the ancient method of allegorical interpretation, but may be exemplified by quoting a modern commentator. "The entrance of light, which itself is real, spreads reality all around. Clouds and shadows are unreal; they breed and foster unrealities. Light is naked truth. . . . It is not seen because it is so pure." Surely, in order to be a good Christian, it is not necessary to eat one's peas with the knife.

John's first Epistle sharply contrasts truth and error, righteousness and sin, light and darkness. The material is controversial and polemic. Some suggest that the object of his attack is Cerinthus, an early heretic who denied the incarnation. This may possibly be so. John and Cerinthus were in a sense contemporaries. At least it is probable that their lives overlapped in time. But rather likely Cerinthus was much younger than John. Some scholars want to date him in the second century. It is also barely possible that John and Cerinthus met, say in Ephesus. But the evidence is less than compelling, and the earlier one dates the Epistle, the less probable it is that John had him in mind. But at any rate, the Epistle attacks some themes Cerinthus later taught.

John's type of writing is widely condemned today in most ecclesiastical circles. Polemics are impolite. We are all brothers in that great fraternity, the mystic Knights of the Sea. Ecumenism has little regard for truth. The still more liberal, or at least the more irrational neo-orthodox have no truth at all. Religion is a nonintellectual encounter, in which 2,000 years of time mysteriously disappear, and we become contemporaneous with Christ. Not only are all ideas permissible in theology, permissiveness allows homosexuals to be ordained to the ministry and condones the murder of unborn infants. If John pressed his polemics today, he would doubtless be boiled in oil a second time. A few small denominations, even if some of them, too, are deteriorating, continue to believe that God is truth and error is sin. This is how John thought and wrote. He begins with "God is light and no darkness is in him at all."

1:6. If we should say that we have fellowship with him and walk in darkness, we lie and do not do the truth.

To support the thesis that what God is determines the conditions of fellowship, Lenski (p. 383) well says:

> To think that we can remain in darkness and yet be in fellowship with him, in whom there is no darkness whatever, is the height [the alliteration as well as the connotation would have been better if Lenski had said *depth*] of delusion, the saddest contradiction. It is elementary, axiomatic: "What communion has light with darkness?" II Cor. 6:14; John 3:19–21.

Some slightly educated Christians, I mean some poorly educated seminary graduates, with or without an attitude of super-devotion, seize upon the phrase "and do not do the truth" in order to make a contrast between the Greek notion of "abstract" truth and the Hebrew emphasis on moral conduct. This is a widespread tactic. Even the radical left-wing Bultmann can say, "In John, truth does not mean the revelatory unveiling of things in the cognitive act, in the Greek sense, but rather the reality of God" (p. 19, col. i). Bultmann ought to know better; but he is warped by his neoorthodox view of personal encounter or confrontation. The more orthodox seminary graduates ought to know better, too, but they have not studied much Greek philosophy. They are warped, and *warped* is the correct word, by their devotion to morality. With such devotion they fallaciously construct a sharp contrast between moral overt action and inner cognitive knowledge. "Cognitive knowledge" is a redundant expression that ought not be necessary. But they hold that morality is practical, while bare, abstract knowledge is not. In this they misconstrue Greek philosophy and the Bible as well.

First, Greek philosophy. A Bible professor recently wrote, in opposition to Greek philosophy and in defense of an ordered providential universe, that Heraclitus pictured the universe as disordered chaos. Nothing could be further from the truth. Heraclitus was the first to propound a Logos-doctrine in which the supreme Deity controlled all events by his wisdom. Further, when "the Greek view" is contrasted with the Hebrew, or biblical, view, these men very frequently assert of all Greek philosophy what is true perhaps of only one author. For example, when Greek "abstract" knowledge is deprecated, do they realize that while Aristotle had a theory of abstraction, Plato denied the possibility of any such mental operation?

I frequently get the impression that these men are so opposed to anything Greek that they reject all geometry because Pythagoras sacrificed a bull to the pagan gods when he discovered his famous theorem. I urge them to construct a Christian theorem that will replace "the square of the length of the hypotenuse of a right triangle equals the sum of the squares of the lengths of the other two sides." To *do the truth* includes learning the truth before criticizing the opponents.

In the next place, the stress these ministers put on practical Christian living in contrast with the Greek abstract impractical concepts is an example of colossal ignorance. Plato began his literary career with dialogues on ethics; he stressed ethics throughout his middle period (*Phaedo, Republic*), and continued on to the *Philebus* and the *Laws* at the end of his life. Aristotle wrote the *Nicomachean Ethics* at least, even if the other two works came from the pens of his students. The Epicureans and the Stoics were fundamentally moral philosophers. The Epicureans based what physics they had on their view of ethics; the Stoics took physics more seriously, but are even today better known for their strict insistence on virtue. To be sure, none of these used Christian criteria to decide between right and wrong, but none of them divorced "abstract" philosophy from practical life.

In the second place, and more unfortunately, these super-devout ministers misunderstand Christianity also, because they think orthodoxy and morality conflict. They do not. It is just the reverse, as this Epistle shows. The doctrine of the Trinity, which is about as "impractical" as any theology can be, is as much a part of Christianity as, "Thou shalt not steal." Indeed this moral commandment would lose all force if the triune God were denied. Atheism cannot logically sustain any morality whatever.[4] Further, if moral truth is to be possible, there must be a theory of truth in general. God is truth; condemn the truth, and morality vanishes. Indeed, the first form of immorality that John here condemns is untruth—telling a lie. But if God were not truth, lying would not be wrong.

> **1:7.   But if we walk in the light as he is in the light, we have fellowship with each other, and the blood of Jesus his Son cleanses us from all sin.**

It is instructive to note how theological doctrine, moral conduct, and fellowship are interlocking rather than divided. Lying is, of course, an overt action opposed to the norms of morality. It also breaks the fellowship. In the previous verse fellowship with God was explicit; in this seventh verse it is fellowship with other Christians. One might have expected John to say, if we walk in the light as God is in the light, we shall have fellowship with God. Obviously true; perhaps too obvious; so John goes one step further and brings in

---

[4]Compare *A Christian View of Men and Things* (Jefferson, Maryland: The Trinity Foundation, 1991 [1952]), chapter IV.

fellowship with one another. But as we have seen and will see still more clearly, all this involves theology as well. The commandments come from God and therefore we must have a correct understanding of him. Lenski says very well, "Ethics are included, but John has in mind first of all doctrine and faith, here false doctrine as opposed to the true. The whole claim to fellowship with God is a lying. John minces no words. Our modern considerateness toward heresies and heretics is unscriptural and dangerous" (p. 387).

Now, every Christian walks in darkness to some extent. We all commit sins. And surely no one can write a commentary without making some mistake in doctrine. All Scripture is profitable for doctrine; but the apostles wrote some things hard to be understood. To this, John adds, "and the blood of Jesus his Son cleanses us from all sin." Making a mistake in a commentary is a sin. All errors in doctrine are sin, and all errors of whatever kind are the result of sin. But the atonement covers them all.

J. R. W. Stott says, "The second result of walking in the light is that the blood of Jesus Christ his Son cleanseth us from all sin." This wording suggests that cleansing from sin is caused by, is the result of, walking in the light. This surely is what John could not possibly mean. We are not cleansed of all sin by moral conduct. We are not cleansed of any sin by moral conduct. If we are honest today, that does not cleanse us of yesterday's dishonesty. And surely it does not cleanse us of all sin. Of course, walking in the light means that we avoid some sins. This is tautological, for walking in the light means to think and act in accordance with God's commandments. To conquer certain sins is by definition to get rid of them. But cleansing from all sin is the work of Christ. His death, his blood, cleanses from all, even though we still commit some. Furthermore, the Greek text does not say *because*, or *is the result of*; the connective is a simple *and*. Two truths are simply conjoined. If our fellowship with God, and other Christians, must wait until our walk cleanses us from all sin, then we shall neither have fellowship nor cleansing in this life.

Roman Catholicism has a scheme of cleansing that goes beyond the blood of Christ. Romanism teaches that Christ's blood is not sufficient to cleanse us. Therefore we must suffer in purgatory. This is anti-Christian. If, as John says, Christ's blood cleanses from all sin, no purgatory is needed. Is not the theology of purgatory a sin? Is it not a lie? Believing the truth is obedience to God; believing false theology is as much a sin as telling a lie about one's age, birthplace, taxable income, or what not.

> My sin—oh the bliss of this wonderful thought—
> My sin, not in part, but the whole
> Is nailed to the cross and I bear it no more.
> Bless the Lord, it is well with my soul.

Calvin in his commentary at this point does not attack the doctrine of purgatory, but rather another popish delusion. He remarks, "Hereby is disproved and exposed the sacrilegious invention of the Papists as to indulgences, for as though the blood of Christ were not sufficient, they add, as a subsidy to it, the blood and merits of martyrs."

1:8. If we should say that we have no sin, we deceive ourselves and the truth is not in us.

There is nothing at all suspicious in this verse, but when we arrive at 3:6 we shall wonder whether John had forgotten 1:8. But though most Christians find nothing suspicious here, there are a few to whom it is embarrassing. I once knew a gentleman of very fine character. Had he been an outrageous sinner, or even a man of only average morality, he would not have served to illustrate the present point. He was indeed an upright, honest, respectable gentleman, and, so far as one can know, a devout Christian. One day he told me and some others, with no trace of pride in his matter of fact tone, "I have not sinned in the last 26 years." He was, obviously, a disciple of John Wesley; and in accordance with his non-Johannine theology he claimed to have achieved sinless perfection. One dislikes to speak evil of so lovely a character; but the plain truth is that the truth was not in him.

He admitted that he had sinned 27 years ago. Maybe some whom John had in mind claimed never to have sinned. But both suffer deception. Most uncomfortably we remember that John in the Gospel applies the phrase "there is no truth in him" to the devil.

Note that the *truth* here is not practical overt action. To be sure, one may vocally claim freedom from sin, and talking is an overt action. But before a man makes the vocal claim, he must have thought so. This thinking, even if not spoken, is falsehood, a lie, absence of truth, and sin. Wesleyan theology is therefore sin because it is not truth. John's statement is entirely universal. He does not say, "Unless we are near death or unless we are very devout, we ought not claim to be sinless." He says "if we say"; and the *we* includes John himself. It is hard to think that John in England (or John in Geneva, who, of course, made no such claim) was holier than John in Ephesus.

Westcott wants to say that "the idea of *planē* [deception] is in all cases that of straying from the one way (James 5:19f.): not of misconception in itself, but of misconduct." This is obviously incorrect. As was just indicated, to think that oneself has no sin, even without saying it, and surely without stealing or committing adultery, is still to deceive oneself. The false thought excludes the truth. It is strange that "practical" Christians except from morality the thinking of a man, since all crimes originate in thought.

1:9.   If we confess our sins, he is faithful and just to forgive us our sins and to cleanse us from all unrighteousness.

Once again John asserts that God cleanses us from all, not just some, unrighteousness. But there is no need for us here to repeat what has been sufficiently said.

The new idea in the verse is the confession of sin. If we have not attained sinless perfection, what is to be done about our daily sins? We must confess. In our prayer we must acknowledge what wrongs we have done, or thought. Confession, too, is "doing the truth," even though private prayer is scarcely overt conduct. Perhaps public prayer, the ministerial or congregational prayer, is overt. But its value depends on inner sincerity, not on sonorous intonation.

Many commentators remark that one must not only confess that in general one is a sinner, or that one inherits original sin from Adam— which David did in Psalm 51:5—but also one must confess particular, concrete, individual sins. This idea is probably the explanation of the plural noun *sins*. In verse 8 *sin* is singular and therefore general. Verse 9 makes it plural and distributive.

This confession must be addressed to God. Verse 9 will make this clearer. It is not addressed to a priest in a cubicle. Bellarmine expresses the Romish view when he says this verse in First John demands confession to a priest. His reason for so interpreting the verse is that it contains a promise of pardon, and that Scripture nowhere promises pardon for confessing to God. All pardon comes through confession to the apostles, and their priestly successors. To which assertion several verses serve as a reply. Leviticus 5:5-6 speaks of a confession, though to whom the confession is made is not stated in verse 5; but verse 6 requires with the confession an offering to the Lord. If this is not quite clear enough, consider Psalm 25:11, "For Thy name's sake O Lord, pardon my iniquity." David confesses to God and asks for pardon. Note that David himself was not a priest, nor did he confess to a priest. As for David, what can the Romanists do with Psalm 51? The opposite of confessing to the Lord is hiding one's sins from him. Isaiah 29:15 says, "Woe to them that seek to hide their counsel from the Lord." The implication is that they should confess to the Lord. In 9:20 Daniel confesses his sin "before the Lord," and not before a priest (cf. Neh. 9:32-34). There are other verses also, if anyone has the energy to look for them. For the sake of a negative completeness it may be mentioned that James 5:16 does not advise confession to a priest. Nor does it advocate house parties at which each one regales the others with a description of his sins. It requires us to acknowledge to another man whatever sin we have committed against him. Certainly "one to another" does not mean "to a priest."

However, permit one more reference. I Kings 8 reports Solomon's prayer at the dedication of the temple. Note well that he was not a priest. Yet he directly asks God for forgiveness (v. 30); he also envisages any ordinary Israelite approaching God to ask for forgiveness (vv. 33, 34, 36). In verse 38 he explicitly uses the words "any man." Now if auricular confession has no place in the Old Testament, how much less in the New! If an Israelite could approach God directly, cannot a humble believer do so also in this age?

There is a second point in the verse that commentators regularly try to explain. The phrase is, "he is faithful and just to forgive us." It is the notion of justice that puzzles some. They expect something like "he is faithful and merciful"; but justice sounds like condemnation. The interpretations, however, do not vary much. God has made many promises. To fail to fulfil them would be unjust. Justice requires forgiveness. Justice in another connection requires an atonement for sin. Behind this verse there is the full doctrine of the atonement. The verse does not deny this. It simply states that "with him there is plenteous redemption."

The final phrase of the verse repeats the final phrase of verse 7: "cleanse us from all unrighteousness."

1:10.   If we should say that we have not sinned, we make him a liar, and his word is not in us.

The translation of this verse, as of most of the preceding, presents no difficulties, except for the translation of *logos*. The English term one chooses is already an interpretation. Here *logos* is translated *word* merely because it is customary.

Verse 8 uses a present tense: "If we should say that we *have* no sin." Here it says, "have not sinned"—the perfect tense. F. F. Bruce claims that "the third false claim is similar to the second but not identical with it." How it differs Bruce does not explain. Lenski says they mean the same thing and then explains how they differ. Is it not better simply to regard the last verse simply as a repetition for emphasis? The emphasis, however, is made clear in the middle phrase. John makes no compromises for the sake of politeness. He uses a more stringent phrase than before, even brutal: we make God a liar. This is strong enough to make us shudder. In view of this condemnation one does not claim sinless perfection. Not only is the concept *liar* a brutal one, but grammatically it is placed in the emphatic position. Greek often emphasizes a word by putting it first in the sentence or phrase. For example, the English translation of Luke 22:33, "I am ready to go with thee, both to prison and to death," might, if the context had warranted it, which it does not, have been an emphasis on "I," Peter, as opposed to the other disciples. But the Greek puts the emphasis on "with thee." A lesser emphasis is on "ready," but "I am" has no emphasis. Here *liar* is the emphatic word; and to think of making God a liar gives us the creeps.

Notice also the final phrase: "his word is not in us." This commentary emphasizes the word because John emphasizes the word. That emphasis is needed today because so much of so-called Christianity is nondoctrinal or antidoctrinal. Theology is in ill repute. But *theo-logy* is the *word* of *God*. The Apostle Paul may have given more detailed expositions of the several doctrines than any other New Testament writer, but no New Testament writer more strongly emphasizes doctrine in general than the Apostle John.

For this reason this commentary aims to explain the meaning of the text, to show the interrelationship of the verses and paragraphs, to facilitate an understanding of the divine message. Earlier it was mentioned that extremely radical critics, who do not accept the message, sometimes interpret it very well. But their view of the whole is so distorted that it is a waste of time to pay much attention to them. To be sure, it is legitimate for a scholar to look at their views and to expose their errors. And even the Christian in the pew will not waste too much time if he examines a sample of their procedures. Hence, follow some paragraphs from Bultmann.

Bultmann does not think that the Epistle is an original production of John. The present text is a compilation from two or more sources: an original source and some other material. We are not interested in all his details, but the following quotations document the preceding sentence. Speaking of I John 1:6–2:17 Bultmann says,

> In this section the author evidently employs a Source which is stylistically related to the Revelatory Discourse Source used in John. The text of the Source, which is commented upon and expanded by the author and by the ecclesiastical redactor, was probably as follows: [Here follows a reconstructed Greek text. A footnote precedes the reconstructed text.] The reconstruction of the putative Source is somewhat different from what I attempted to give in [another book]. There I showed by stylistic features that differentiate the author from the Source, the difference between the Source and the additions of the author. Here I only point to the fact that the sentences of the Source form parallel members. . . . In distinction from the prosaic style of the author, the language of the Source can be characterized as poetical.

On page 19, with reference to the words "with one another," he says, "One might expect 'fellowship with him' in accordance with v. 6. In all likelihood, that is what stood in the conjectured Source, but the author of the Epistle probably changed it to 'with one another.' " Then on page 20, column 2, he says, "Before the conjectured Source is again taken up in v. 8, a sentence is inserted in v. 7b, which is probably an addition of the ecclesiastical redactor." The general idea of all this is that the Epistle began as a treatise in some unknown source. Then the author of the Epistle altered this to suit himself; and after him an ecclesiastical editor made insertions, subtractions, or other changes. The argument is based on style and wording: the author could not have used this word, he had to use that one, and the editor used a different word.

Two things may be said to all this. First, Lutoslawski, a Polish Platonic scholar, studied the changing style of Plato from his earliest dialogues to his latest. In this way he could determine approximate dates for several of the dialogues. But note: he had hundreds of pages of Platonic writing. John's Epistle has scarcely a dozen. Further, Lutoslawski determined relative dates: not insertions, deletions, alterations. Second, the style of Nietzsche's *Thus Spake Zarathustra* and his *Ecce Homo* are unmistakably different; but no one concludes they were written by different authors.

At this point the conclusion is that Bultmann's method is entirely subjective and conjectural. He has no objective evidence to make his views even plausible. Though they are not worth considering, a further example will be given in 3:8. It will surely justify the witty and scathing satire that follows.

After this interlude the reader may have forgotten what John was saying. Even without the interlude he may have seen more leaves than trees. Since there is a logical break at the end of chapter 1, it will be appropriate to summarize, outline, and perhaps anticipate chapter 2. Some repetition cannot be avoided.

A. The Condition of Righteousness   1:5–2:6
   1. Confession of Sin   1:5–2:2
      i. Since God is Light, we must walk in the light, i.e., be cleansed by the blood of Christ.   1:5–7
     ii. Since we are sinners, we must confess. If we do, God forgives us. If we do not, we call God a liar.   1:8–10

If it were not for the interlude on Bultmann, we would not have stopped here, but would have continued on to the main break, *viz.*

     iii. Forgiveness comes from our advocate and propitiation, Jesus Christ.   2:1–2

The Second Chapter

2:1   My children, I am writing these things to you that you may not sin. And even if someone sins, we have an advocate with the Father, Jesus Christ, [the] just [one].

TO whom did John write? Paul's Epistles are addressed to churches at Rome, Corinth, Thessalonica, and so on, or to individuals, Titus and Timothy. But John's letter is addressed to nobody. Paul signed his letters. So did Jude, James, and Peter. But here no proper name appears except that of Jesus Christ. The letter may have been sent to the seven churches of Asia Minor, or to one or two of them. It is plausible to assume that his immediate addressees were mainly his own converts because of the phrase "my children." We cannot suppose that John founded these churches. Paul preceded him in Ephesus. But sometime after the destruction of Jerusalem John came to Ephesus and remained in the vicinity until his death in about A.D. 100. The tone of the Epistle is that of a well-known, loving, and beloved father. This makes it unlikely that the Epistle was written before, say, the year 80. But though there is no certainty as to his immediate addressees, that is to which or how many congregations he sent the letter, we know that the Holy Spirit addressed the letter to all Christians in every land and every age.

It is possible also to infer that since the Christians of John's day were his children, a contemporary minister is the father of his congregation. Protestants do not much care for the Roman Catholic usage of "Father"; and the short length of pastorates, which in recent years has degraded the pastor into an administrator, or into a semiprofessional counselor, is not conducive to fatherly responsibilities. But Paul, as well as John, was a father.

John's purpose in addressing Christians was to encourage them not to sin. The Jews in the time of Paul attacked the doctrine of justification by faith alone on the ground that it encouraged sinning. To this objection Paul wrote Romans 6-8. Here also, but more briefly, John strongly discourages sinning. There is no logical incompatibility between justification and sanctification. But though the logic is so clear, and the apostles' replies so ancient, the same objections recur today in befuddled minds. The Epistle is pertinent today.

Minds are befuddled by sin. Adam before the fall may have been ignorant of many things, but his original righteousness guaranteed him against any blunder in logic. Sin then disturbed his mind. So today people may argue: sinless perfection is impossible, therefore it is useless and foolish to try to achieve it, therefore I shall be content to sin every now and then. This is a plausible argument. But a flaw may be found in it. Indeed, sinless perfection in this life is an unattainable goal. But progress toward that goal is not impossible. The goal defines the direction. Suppose a student wants to become a great mathematician. He not only wants to prove the Fermat theorem, but to go far beyond it. Yet presumably he realizes that he cannot exhaust the future possibilities of mathematics. Does he then conclude that he will be satisfied with a blunder now and then? He knows very well that he will make blunders; but he never ceases trying to avoid them.

Since the apostle knows that Christians will commit sins, he adds "if anyone sins, we have an advocate with the Father." *Paraklētos* is distinctly a legal term. Etymologically it means someone called to aid; and a few commentators emphasize that the word thus has a passive meaning: someone called, not someone who calls. This is not terribly significant. What is more so is that a *paraklētos* is called to aid in a court of law. He is an attorney, a lawyer. The verb *paraklēteuō* means to act as an advocate or intercessor. There is a good reason for noting this in our contemporary situation. Many religious persons complain that justification, federal headship, guilt and punishment, are legal concepts, and that legality is antithetical to grace and a religion of love. Thus these people undermine the Christian gospel. Note that sin is defined by God's law, as John will say in a few verses further on, and as Paul makes so very clear. There is nothing sub-

Christian in legality. God is a law-giver. Christians are obligated to obey the law. They have no right (and right is also a legal term) to murder, commit adultery, or steal. Christ never abrogated the Ten Commandments. The New Testament says that if we offend in one point, we are guilty of all. And from Matthew to Revelation there are warnings of God's great judgment theme. The gospel is not an antinomian device for encouraging sin. Could any language to this effect have greater clarity than John's?

But we do sin, nevertheless. Then what? Shall we delay baptism until a minute before we die and trust the water to wash away our sins? Some early Christians (if indeed, they were Christians—at least they thought they were) held this view.

On the contrary, John said, we have a lawyer in the Judge's court-room. He is not a shyster, but a just advocate. He knows how to plead. Westcott is as wrong as anyone can be when he wrote, "Nothing is said of the manner of Christ's pleading: that is a subject wholly beyond our powers." One should not infer that Westcott never says anything good. Even Bultmann stumbles into something good once in a while; and Bultmann is far worse than Westcott. But there is a frequent and very irritating tendency abroad in religious circles to assume a false humility of ignorance in order to evade the clear teaching of Scripture. No doubt Westcott is less guilty on this point than many others. But nonetheless we insist that it is false to say *"nothing* is said of the manner of Christ's pleading: that is a subject *wholly* beyond our powers." The very next verse says something extremely important. True, not everything is said in the next verse; but the most important thing is said. As an introduction to verse 2, the thought of another author can well be substituted for Westcott's remark. In fact, the idea is so well expressed that it demands reproduction in full.

> Arise, my soul, arise, Shake off thy guilty fears:
> The bleeding Sacrifice In my behalf appears:
> Before the Throne my Surety stands,
> My name is written on his hands.
>
> He ever lives above, For me to intercede,
> His all-redeeming love, His precious blood to plead;
> His blood atoned for every race,
> And sprinkles now the throne of grace

Five bleeding wounds he bears, Received on Calvary;
They pour effectual prayers, They strongly plead for me;
Forgive him, O forgive, they cry,
Nor let that ransomed sinner die!

My God is reconciled; His pard'ning voice I hear;
He owns me for his child, I can no longer fear;
With confidence I now draw nigh,
And "Father, Abba, Father!" cry.

**2:2.   And he is the *hilasmos* for our sins; not for our sins
only, but also for all the world.**

The translation: The important word here is *hilasmos*. This Greek
word was clearly understood and correctly translated in times past.
But recently bad translations have been foisted on the public. Therefore, it is necessary to consult the dictionaries. If this is tedious, it is
nevertheless of extreme importance. The best Greek-English lexicon
is that of Liddell and Scott (xlviii + 2111 pages). *Hilaskomai*, the
verb, means

> . . . *appease*, in Homer always of gods, . . . of men *conciliate*. 3. *expiate*
> . . . to be merciful, gracious . . . *Hilasma*, propitiation . . . *hilasmos*,
> a means of appeasing. 2. atonement, sin-offering. *hilastērios*, propitia-
> tory, offered in propitiation. . . . II *hilastērion*, the mercy seat . . .
> propitiatory gift or offering. 3. monastery. *hilastēs*, propitiator.

Probably the next best Greek-English lexicon, a lexicon of Hellenistic Greek, is that of Arndt and Gingrich, who translated and added
to the German lexicon of Walter Bauer. It says, "*hilaskomai*, propitiate, conciliate (god, gods). Pass. be propitiated, be merciful or
gracious . . . 2. expiate . . . *hilasmos*, expiation, propitiation (the
gods) . . . 2. sin-offering.

J. R. W. Stott (pp. 84–85) does not depend on two lexicons, but
surveys the modern translations and also summarizes an excellent
analysis of the term by Leon Morris. The latter successfully cuts the
ground from under the liberal attempts to rid the Old Testament of
the idea of propitiation. In doing so, he examines the terminology of
the Greek Septuagint. Stott and Morris completely refute Dodd and
other moderns, and establish the correct English translation.

With the support especially of the Septuagint, the present commentary restricts itself to noting that in both the two great lexicons the main meaning is *propitiate;* and both indicate that the object of the propitiation is God, or the gods. It may be possible to propitiate, or at least conciliate men, but the most frequent reference is to the gods. One will also note that both lexicons list *expiate* as a secondary or tertiary meaning.

This raises the problem, not so much of translation narrowly conceived, but of the always overlapping concern for good English. Now, Merriam Webster lists propitiation as a *synonym* of expiation. It also lists expiation as a synonym of propitiation. However, it seems that these two words are not exact synonyms and are not interchangeable. Let the reader ask himself, Would I say God is expiated and sins propitiated? The present writer thinks that these two phrases are both inappropriate. Surely God is propitiated and sins expiated.

As evidence of English usage let us quote John Cotton. "Some translations render it, 'He is the reconciliation;' but that does not express the full meaning. Propitiation includes three things. (1) It requires that he should expiate our sins, that is, make satisfaction for them. A man may be a means of reconciliation without satisfaction, but he cannot be a propitiation without satisfaction."

Bultmann has no trouble with this passage. "The ecclesiastical redactor has appended v. 2. . . . This thought, however, does not agree with v. 1, . . . The concept of *hilasmos* (expiation), which is also foreign to the Gospel of John, belongs to the ecclesiastical theology."

It is also noted that in Hebrews 2:17 the verb *hilaskesthai* has *sins* as its object. No one translates this "to propitiate sins." But if expiation and propitiation were synonymous, the latter would be proper. The present commentator is therefore compelled to regard the phrase in Hebrews as an abbreviation of the idea of propitiating God for the expiation of sins. He must also repudiate and repudiate emphatically any version of the New Testament which avoids the term *propitiation* in I John or Romans 3:25. I insist that the RSV translation of I John 1:2 is absolutely wrong. The irresponsible *Good News for Modern Man* is worse. The NIV suffers from a very serious defect. It says "atoning sacrifice for our sins" both here and in the other verses where the Greek term occurs. The serious defect consists, not merely in choosing a poor phrase, but rather that the phrase is poor because it obscures, in effect, deletes, the true meaning.

Suppose a man, his wife, and two small children are vacationing in a small cabin north of the Tetons and south of Yellowstone. Early one morning as the aroma of eggs and bacon fills the cabin, the wife looks out the window and calls to her husband, "There's an animal at our front door." This is not just what the husband wants to hear. If the animal is a deer, the father would take the children to the window to see it. But if it is a grizzly, attracted by frying bacon, he would do something else. True enough, an animal is there; but the safety of the family depends on what animal it is. Or if you are in the Black Hills, and a snake crawls into your hut, you want to know immediately whether it is a gopher snake or a rattlesnake. The simple word *snake* is dangerously inappropriate.

Similarly "an atoning sacrifice for sin" is dangerously vague. All sorts of rituals can be called atoning sacrifices. But salvation, in the Christian sense of the term, requires one very definite type of sacrifice, namely, a propitiation. John is not at all so vague as the New International Version. He is perfectly specific. Christ's atoning sacrifice is a propitiation. Its aim was to appease the wrath of an angry God; and it succeeded in doing so.

Stott, in the material referred to above points out the reason why present day scholars change the translations:

> The main contemporary objection to the vocabulary of "propitiation" is theological. It is said to conjure up notions of an irritable and capricious deity who needs to be appeased with bribes. Such ideas are rightly dismissed as pagan and inconsistent with the revelation of God in Jesus Christ. Apparently unwilling to concede that there may be a biblical and Christian concept of propitiation quite distinct from crude pagan views, some scholars proceed to support their theological rejection of propitiation with linguistic arguments. (p. 85)

Now, it is doubtful that the Greek gods were as capricious as Stott seems to think. The spheres of their interests were fairly well defined and the sacrifices were not usually aimed at getting them to violate their prerogatives. They were not exactly bribes. The Apostle Paul indeed says that the Greek gods, Zeus, Artemis, Poseidon, k.t.l. are nothing, and that the Greeks sacrifice to demons. So be it. But in criticizing Greek religion, we must center upon what the Greeks thought; and the Greeks did not view them as mainly capricious. It is also possible that Christians who denounce the Greek gods as capricious may infringe on the sovereignty of the God of Abraham, Isaac, and Jacob, who often looks capricious to non-Christians. Why did God choose Abraham? Why did God choose Judas? For a purpose, assuredly. But the pagan gods had purposes, too. Instead of depending on a contemporary dislike of caprice, why not stress the non-Christian character of pagan purposes? In combatting a non-Christian system one should try to be as accurate as possible. To picture an opponent as worse than he is, or even other than he is, backfires. Now, the Greek religions were polytheistic. There is no question on that score. Therefore, one may point out that polytheism allows for no sovereignty. There is no unified rule throughout the world. Zeus may be greater than any of the others, but he is not omnipotent. Nor is there any idea of creation. All these are legitimate points of criticism. So, too, the morals of the gods: their conduct was not superior to that of average mortals. In these matters a Christian has legitimate grounds for criticism.

It also seems that Stott's phrase about modern scholars, who are "unwilling to concede that there may be a biblical and Christian concept of propitiation" is too weak. These modern scholars are antagonistic to all forms of propitiation. They insist that propitiation in the Bible is as objectionable as propitiation in Homer. Some of them find the source of the idea in pagan rituals worse than those of Homer. Qualify Christian propitiation as you please, these men reject every notion of a God of wrath, justice, and anger. Any sugar coating only disguises the poisonous pill.

But the Bible reveals a God of wrath and justice. Any person may honestly hold a contrary opinion; but no one can honestly deny that such is what the Bible teaches. "O generation of vipers, who hath warned you to flee from the wrath to come?" "He that believeth not the Son shall not see life; but the wrath of God abideth on him." "The wrath of God is revealed from heaven against all ungodliness of men who hold [or, hold down] the truth in [or, by] unrighteousness." There are nearly three dozen references to the wrath of God in the New Testament. Hence the method of atonement must be satisfaction and propitiation. To talk about an animal instead of a grizzly is to obscure the gospel in its entirety.

There are two other verbal points in this verse, one of which still has to do with the term *hilasmos*. Most commentators correctly note that Christ is not said to be the *propitiator*, but the *propitiation*. Now, it is true enough that Christ was the propitiator, our great High Priest, who offered a sacrifice to God. But more than this, and in stark distinction from the high priests from Moses on, Jesus was the *propitiation*. That is, he was not only the sacrificer; he was the sacrifice. The earlier priests sacrificed lambs. Jesus sacrificed himself. The second verbal point emphasizes this. The word *himself* is the second word in the verse. "And *himself*." This demonstrative pronoun adds emphasis. It is a point not to be missed. Jesus was not only the priest; he himself was also the lamb—the Lamb of God that taketh away the sin of the world. In theological language, which is usually much clearer than colloquial speech, this is called the vicarious or substitutionary sacrifice. As the lamb suffered death instead of the Old Testament saints, so Christ bore the penalty instead of our bearing it. Liberals and atheists may repudiate all this and invent whatever religion pleases them; but no competent scholar can deny that this is what the Bible teaches, and what the Bible teaches is Christianity. Anything else is not.

The next phrase of verse 2 is, "not for our sins only, but also for all the world."

One or two commentators note that John, in the last phrase, does not say "for the sins of the whole world." At least one insists that John's words are not a condensed expression for "the sins of the whole world." But it is hard to see what other meaning the phrase could have. Propitiation makes sense only on a background of sin.

Now, if Christ propitiated God in the sense of having expiated the sins of every human being, past, present, and future, it would follow that God is no longer at enmity with anyone. Everyone is at peace with God. No one is lost; there is no hell; all sins have been pardoned; and Hitler and Stalin will sit down together at the marriage supper of the Lamb.

This not only contradicts Matthew and Revelation. It ill accords with the present Epistle. Later we shall arrive at 2:18, 19; 3:10; 4:3; and 5:16. However, the present verse must be discussed first.

The Arminian argument, which though fallacious seems plausible, runs about as follows. In this and other passages Christ is said to be the Savior of the world. These passages, with one exception, are all found in John's writings. John never uses the term *world* to denote the elect only. He rather uses it to designate the wicked in opposition to the righteous. Therefore, the present verse means that Jesus' death propitiates the Father both with respect to Christians and pagans.

This argument is plausible, especially if one does not examine the pertinent passages throughout the New Testament, including those in the Gospel. Unfortunately, many people do not examine them; at most they read them carelessly. Fewer people are any longer acquainted with the great Puritan writings, which were the glory of the seventeenth century. Then it was that Protestantism, Evangelicalism, Calvinism reached its zenith. Of course, there were Arminians in those days, too. A famous one was Dr. Whitby, and his *Discourse on the Five Points*. In 1735 John Gill, a great (shall I say the greatest) Baptist theologian published *The Cause of God and Truth*. In it he exegeted all the verses Dr. Whitby used, including I John 2:2. His examination of the verse is too long to quote in a book like this; but the following is a faithful, if not complete, summary.

First, he points out that the word *world* has several meanings in John's writings (and, I may add, a few more in other New Testament books). Since there are clearly several meanings, it follows that the meaning in one passage is not necessarily the meaning in another. Each passage must be studied in its context. Sometimes *world* signifies the whole universe of created beings, as in John 1:10, including rocks, trees, planets, and human beings. In John 16:28 it means the inhabitable earth. John 15:19 uses the word to designate unconverted people. Some of these could later be converted; but in John 17:9 the *world* is that group of sinners who are so wicked that Jesus does not even pray for them.

Perhaps an Arminian will charge Gill with begging the question in his next reference. Gill says that John 1:29 uses the word *world* for the elect alone. It more clearly means the elect in John 6:33, for the reference is to those who have life by eating the bread from heaven. This is borne out in verse 35. See also 6:51. John 12:19 uses the term *world* to designate those people who followed after Jesus. It is true that these are the words of the Pharisees; but they show what the word *world* can mean. Gill particularly notes that these people form an exceedingly small proportion of the human race. (The usage is similar to the French phrase *tout le monde,* or the common English term *everybody,* when only a few are meant.)

Returning to John 1:10, Gill notes that the *world* occurs three times, each time with a different meaning: Christ was in the habitable *earth,* and the whole *universe* was made by him, and the *greater part* of humanity did not know him.

At this point Gill's conclusion is:

> the word *world* is always used in John's writings in a restricted and limited sense, for some only, unless when it designates the whole universe or habitable earth, senses which are not out of the question, for none will say Christ died for the sun, moon, and stars, for fishes, fowls, brutes, sticks, and stones; and that it is never used to signify every individual of mankind that has been, is, or shall be in the world; in which sense it ought to be proved it is used, if any argument can be concluded from it in favor of general redemption.[1]

The second part of Gill's argument goes beyond the determination of a single word, and proceeds into more extensive exegesis.

After having made the point that the *world,* when used in conjunction with ideas of redemption, never means every human being, Gill considers John 1:29, "Behold the Lamb of God which taketh away the sins of the world." This cannot possibly mean that Christ takes away the sins of every individual man, for the clear reason that Scripture refers to some who die in their sins, whose sins go beforehand to judgment, for which they will be righteously and everlastingly condemned. Yet they would not suffer everlastingly if Christ had taken away their sins.

Then there is the verse which is probably the best known verse in the Bible: John 3:16. "God so loved the world. . . ." The term *world* cannot mean every son and daughter of Adam. The reason is that the *world* here intended is the object of God's love, indeed of his special redeeming love, to the extent that they shall never perish; and this group does not include every person on the face of the earth. The people intended are those for whom God has given his only begotten Son, in fact those to whom God has given the power to believe; but not all men have this faith. Those whom Christ came to save will never perish; the others will, for these shall die the second death.

---

[1]The last long clause, beginning with "it is never used," seems solidly founded on Scripture. However, while sun, stars, stones, and animals are never redeemed from sin, for they are sinless, nonetheless the death of the Creator is so stupendous that it must have some effect on the lower creation. The earth was cursed because of Adam's sin, and in the end the earth shall be burned up and its elements melt with a fervent heat; so that

> No more let sins and sorrows grow,
> Nor thorns infest the ground.

The words in the following verse corroborate this. With the same thought elsewhere expressed John 3:17 says that Christ did not come to condemn the world, but to save it. Obviously the world he saved was the elect. If Christ were the Savior of every individual, he would be the Savior of both believers and unbelievers. This is contrary to his own declaration, "He that believeth and is baptized shall be saved, he that believeth not shall be damned."

When Christ says, "The bread of God is he that cometh down from heaven and giveth life to the world," no more can be designed by the *world* than those to whom this bread of God gives life. But it is clear that God does not give life to everyone.

Somewhat in desperation an Arminian may now object, if the *world* does not include everyone, surely in I John 2:2, the verse now under discussion, the *whole* world must designate every last individual. Surely the phrase *the whole world* admits of no exception.

This argument is based on an ignorance of Hebrew. Here Gill cites five instances in which *the whole world* designates not merely a fraction of the earth's population but a fraction of the Jewish nation.

But aside from Hebrew usage, the New Testament does not mean every individual when it says *"the whole world."* Luke 2:1 is an instance. (Strictly this verse says, "all the inhabited land," whereas the Epistle says "the whole cosmos." Yet Caesar Augustus' decree was limited in extent. It went to all the Empire, but not to inhabited China.) Paul said that the faith of the Roman church was spoken of in the whole cosmos. But not in China. In fact, it probably means in all the Christian churches. Romans 3:19 says "that all the cosmos should become guilty before God." Of course, this does not refer to the moon, sun, and planets. Nor (possibly) to all human beings. Assuming that "the law" in the preceding verses means the Mosaic law, Gill says that only those under the Mosaic law could in this way become guilty, and not "all mankind, who though all guilty by the law of nature, yet not by the law of Moses." Revelation 3:10 speaks of a temptation that will come upon the whole inhabited earth. This cannot mean all the men and women who have ever lived, but only those who happen to be alive at that time. Gill then adds a few more cases to prove that *all the world* never means every son and daughter of Adam. One of these is in the present Epistle: I John 5:19. We shall comment on it when we get into chapter 5; but here it is proper to continue with the subject at hand. The verse says, "We know that we are of God, and the whole cosmos lieth in wickedness." Clearly the "whole world" excludes the righteous. The "world" is not every human being, but only the wicked.

Now, the Arminians, who want a universal propitiation, are obliged to show that the "world" means every individual that has been, is, or will be. This they cannot do. The Scripture is uniformly opposed to their way of thinking.

With all this scriptural background it is time to return to the verse at hand. The verse distinguishes between "our sins" and the "sins of the whole world." Therefore, as in the later verse, John does not include us in the "whole world." Furthermore, a propitiation propitiates. If Christ propitiates the Father for every human being, then every human being will be saved. But the Bible rules out universalism. Enforcing this is the point that the propitiation is effective through faith in Christ's blood, as Romans 3:25 says. God's anger is not appeased in the case of unbelievers. There again, while Christ is the advocate, or trial lawyer, for us, as the previous verse indicates (first person plural, *echomen*, referring to *my little children*), he is not the lawyer for the reprobate. And as the Gospel says, Christ does not pray for, or advocate the cause of, those others. Indeed, if Christ were the advocate of every human being, including those who are now in hell, and those who will be, what comfort can it be to us that he is our propitiation? His work was ineffective in those cases, why not then in ours?

In what sense then can Christ be the propitiation for the sins of the whole world? First, we should note that John was a Jew, and probably of a priestly family. It is also likely that at the early date of the Epistle the congregations or congregations to whom John wrote were still largely Jewish. Now, it is incontestable that Jewish writers referred to the Gentiles as "the world." The rabbis argued as to whether the blessings of the Messiah, when he should come, would extend beyond the Jews to the world. There were many negative votes. Hence there is no reason to deny, and enough support to assert, that when John speaks of the world he means the Gentiles as opposed to the Jews. This, then, is the meaning of I John 2:2, and the conclusion of the summary of John Gill's exegesis.

2:3.   And by this we know [at the present moment] that we have known [and continue to know] him, if we keep his commandments.

In the outline, 1:5–2:6 was labeled "The Condition of Righteousness" under which there were two points: (1) Confession of sin, and (2) Actual obedience. Verse 2:3 begins this second point. The thought of the verse has been slightly anticipated. The idea of an advocate raised the question of legalism. So here also, obedience to commandments has a legalistic sound. And, of course, legalism is bad, very bad, utterly contrary to grace, isn't it?

In religion, as in politics, the last few decades have seen a sometimes deliberate, sometimes unwitting debasement and misuse of language. The terms *evangelical, born again,* political *liberal,* and *human life,* have lost their original meaning. So, too, the term *legalism* in theology. Legalism used to mean the theory that by doing good works a man can earn his entrance into heaven. Today it is used to belittle basic morality. To refrain from violating the Ten Commandments is legalism. Joseph Fletcher advises Christians to break every one of them. The idea that grace abolishes law, and the idea that justification by faith alone encourages licentiousness, were disposed of by Paul in Romans. John does the same thing. But people who advocate premarital sex, promiscuity, who exclude the Bible from public schools and try to prevent the operation of Christian schools, praise freedom and denounce law and order. When Christians, or professing Christians, do some of these things, they talk of grace and oppose 'legalism.'

There was a young department head working at a Sears store. He was a member of a very fundamentalistic church. At a certain date Sears started doing business on Sunday. My friend told me that he was disturbed at first, but he prayed about it, and God told him it was all right to work on Sunday. There was also a very fundamentalistic minister who came to the conclusion he should first cheat on his wife, then divorce her, and marry his paramour. Why get married? That is legalism, too.

Probably the many loose women in the United States do not pray very much. But if some do, they will probably tell us that God approves the slaughter of millions of babies.

John says that it is by keeping God's laws that we can know that we know Christ. Assurance of salvation is a topic John considers in several sections of this Epistle. It is possible to consider this the main subject throughout. One could say that our standing with God is tested by righteousness, love, and doctrine, and these three, repeated, give grounds for assurance. Some of the material, for example 1:6-10, is either negative, that is, proofs that one is not a Christian, or a bit too general and inclusive to be labeled a specific argument on assurance. But the present verse is neither too general and vague, nor negative. It says positively that we can know we know Christ by obeying the commandments.

There is a difficulty, however, that should be honestly faced. In his earlier days Luther tried to obey God and satisfy his demands; but he was never sure that he had done enough. This haunting fear led him into asceticism. Now, having been instructed by him in the evangelical doctrine of justification by faith, we today can easily avoid some Romish misconceptions. Nevertheless, we know all too well that we do not keep God's commandments as we should. How sanctified must we become before we pass from timid hope to bold assurance? If the main purpose of this Epistle is to teach assurance—this may be inferred from 1:4, because our joy can be full only if we have assurance; though there are so many ideas in the Epistle that it is hard to speak of just one main purpose—or at least one of John's purposes is to teach assurance, we must apply his criteria to ourselves and ask if we measure up.

2:4.   He who says, I have known him, and does not keep his commandments, is a liar, and in such a person the truth does not exist.

It is not really a matter of translation, for *pseustēs* clearly means liar; but the etymology tempts us to write "pseudo-Christian." At any rate the verse indicates that some people say "I know him," when as a matter of fact they do not. We may well doubt the sincerity of a politician who claims to be born again, but who uses his powers to favor abortion. In such a person, the truth does not reside. Lenski's words are as plain as John's:

> The man who claims, "I have known God," and does not keep God's commandments is nothing but a plain liar, not merely because his

claim and his conduct disagree and contradict each other, his conduct giving the lie to his claim, nor because he just fails to see this and is thus only a sadly *mistaken* liar—no, far worse, he is a *deliberate* liar: "in this one the truth is not."

There is a good reason for asserting that the disobedient man does not believe the truth. The reason is that intellectual conviction inevitably controls action. As a man thinketh in his heart, so is he; for out of the heart are the issues of life. A man may not openly express his conviction; indeed, he may assert opinions he does not hold in order to deceive his associates. But eventually his actions will reveal what he really thought. Hence, by simple logical conversion, if a man disobeys God's commandments, it follows that he does not know God. Our actions, as the result of our beliefs, reveal what we believe. As the old, tried and true cliche says, actions speak louder than words.

But this is very disturbing, for all of us disobey God's commands. Can we then be assured that we have been regenerated? Maybe our faith is pseudo.

Some commentators stress the need for moral obedience to the divine commands. Murder, adultery, and theft are not Christian behavior. And this is true, very true. But in their strong insistence on overt moral action (preserving physical life, family life, and private property), some of these commentators fail to note that God commands certain intellectual activities. Obedience is not always overt. We must also *think* or *believe* the truth. In his Gospel, John quotes Christ, "If anyone maintains my *doctrine*, he shall not see death, ever." It must be insisted that overt moral action can be the result only of correct doctrine. But the twentieth century is more enamoured with existential titillation than with objective truth.

2:5.   But whoever maintains his doctrine, truly in him the love of God has been perfected. By this we know that we are in him.

Translation: A few lines above the term *logos* in John 8:51 was translated *doctrine*. So also here. The Greek term *logos* can mean a word, such as *cat* or *dog*. But this meaning is extremely rare. Matthew 15:23 does indeed indicate that Jesus did not utter a single word; though had he spoken, it would have probably been a complete sentence. To find an instance in classical or Hellenistic Greek would require a time consuming search. Maybe an instance could be found, but almost always *logos* does not mean a *word*. The more common meanings, in classical, Hellenistic, and Koinē Greek are: an *audit* of financial accounts; the *accounts* themselves; *esteem* and *consideration;* the *value* put on a person or thing; *refute;* a mathematical *ratio* or *proportion;* an *explanation; plea,* or *pretext; purpose* or *reason;* a *theory* or *argument;* a *principle* or *law;* a *formula* or *definition;* a generative *principle* in nature (Stoic); a *debate; deliberation;* a *narrative* or *fiction,* or even *slander; discussion;* divine *utterance* or *oracle; proverb, maxim,* or *saying; speech, sentence,* or *language;* and a dozen or more related meanings. No apology is needed for translating *logos* as *doctrine.* Most of the time it makes much better sense than the word *word.*

John, therefore, teaches that if anyone holds to the divine doctrine, in him is the love of God truly perfected.

Almost all commentators ask whether "the love of God" is a subjective or objective genitive. The words themselves do not decide the question. One must seek the sense. Is our love of God perfected by our advance in theological truth; or is God's love for us so perfected? First, let us note the phrase as it occurs in the remainder of the Epistle. In 2:15 the genitive seems to be objective (i.e., God is the object of the Christian's loving) by reason of the parallelism with the first half of the verse. It is possible, though less likely, that by a chiastic reversal, the word "God" could be a subjective genitive (i.e. God's love for us). There is no genitive in 3:1, but the love mentioned there is the Father's loving us. Verse 16 of the same chapter is clearly subjective: God showed his love for us. Verse 17 is doubtful, but most people would consider it objective: our love for God. Genitives occur also in 4:7, 9, but they occur with a preposition. Not only the preposition but the clear meaning of 4:9 leaves no doubt that it is God who does the loving. So also, and very definitely, verses 10, 11, possibly 12, and certainly 16. The objective sense (our love toward God) is clear in 5:3, both because of the verse itself, and especially because of the preceding context. John's preponderant usage is the subjective genitive; in fact, this is the more common usage in the New Testament as a whole; but this alone does not settle the meaning in 2:5. It may, however, warn us not to conclude too hastily that the genitive in 2:5 is an objective genitive.

That the love referred to here is man's love for God seems at first to make better sense because while there is no difficulty in conceiving this human love to grow and become more perfect, it is hard to conceive of an inferior divine love improving as time passes. Nevertheless, if the difficulty just mentioned can be avoided, the other interpretation will be the better one. And the difficulty can be avoided. It is not a matter of God's love becoming more perfect in itself than it ever was. But rather this love by God has the aim of blessing and sanctifying man. In the course of time God's love accomplishes its purpose more fully. In the Christian who maintains God's truth, God's love has truly come to fruition. F. F. Bruce, J. R. W. Stott, and the RSV take the opposite view. Lenski agrees with the present writer, or vice versa.[2]

The last phrase of the verse is, "By this we know that we are in him." Sometimes it is difficult to decide whether "By this" refers to what John has just said, or refers to what he is about to say. Here clearly he refers to what he has just said. The KJV punctuation, contrary to Stott's assertion that it is wrong, is the correct interpretation; and most of the contemporary versions, including the NIV, ignore the parallel context and damage the sense. In verse 3 "by this" refers to what follows. The thought continues through verse 5. It all refers to keeping God's commandments and maintaining his truth. The present phrase refers to what precedes it and so closes the thought of these three verses. Then verse 6 adds a concluding remark about Jesus' own conduct, an idea not found in the preceding. Note the sense: John wishes us to know that we are in Christ. Now, we do not know that we are in Christ *because* a Christian ought to walk as Christ walked. We know we are in Christ because we maintain his doctrine. Verse 6 is an added thought, and cannot be the reason for verse 5. F. F. Bruce, as well as Stott, misses the point. Lenski has it right. *Mirabile dictu,* Bultmann agrees.

The phrase "we are in him" is an interesting one. The first *him* in verse 3 refers to Christ; and the second *him* should also refer to Christ, for he gave commandments as well as the Father. So, also, in verse 4. But do these repeated references to commandments begin to shift our

---

[2]The embarrassment of agreeing with Bultmann also is mitigated by the remainder of his interpretation.

attention toward the Father? At any rate, verse 5 speaks of God; and therefore the *him* at the end of the verse may mean the Father rather than Christ.

Someone may say it makes no difference. In the context that is the case. Nevertheless, there is a difference between being in Christ and being in God. Acts 17:28 teaches that all men, heathen as well as Christians, live, move, and have their being in God. Stranger still, John himself, not Paul, says that Christ is the light of all men. This light, however, is epistemological and not soteric. In the Epistle, the phrase "in him" (and it more likely means Christ, for that better fits the next verse) is clearly soteric. John is concerned with salvation, even the assurance of salvation.

The metaphorical phrase "to be in Christ" occurs in several contexts. It may mean obedience to a specific command, as in I Corinthians 7:39 where a widow is free to marry a second time, but only in the Lord. It also refers to a wider range of conduct, for, put negatively, every branch in me that beareth no fruit, he taketh away. Ephesians 1:4 speaks of the saints as being in Christ before the foundation of the world—proleptically, we must say. Paul in Romans 16:7 mentions Andronicus and Junia "who were in Christ before me"; they were not elected before him but regenerated before him. Since the context in I John does not mention election, the phrase here means regeneration. The theme has been assurance.

2:6.   He who says he abides in him ought himself to walk as that one walked.

"That one" obviously is Christ, and this bears on the meaning of the preceding pronouns. This verse is an exhortation, or at least a statement of obligation. Therefore, as was argued above, it is not a reason for assurance. It is an additional thought used as a closing "punch line." The reader is expected to say to himself: Certainly if I am in Christ, I ought to walk as Christ walked. That it is a concluding remark is also evidenced by the fact that it repeats the idea with which the chapter began: I write to you in order that you may not sin. To attach it to verse 5 instead of to verse 1 destroys the symmetry of the paragraph.

The verb *abide* or *remain* comes from the lips of Jesus himself (six) times in John 15); it precludes any idea of being in again out again, saved at breakfast, lost by noon, and resaved by supper. It connotes permanence rather than emotional ups and downs. This is the way Christ walked. He set his face stedfastly, as Luke 9:51 says, toward Jerusalem. There was no wavering. So ought we also to walk as that one walked.

2:7.   Beloved, I do not write to you a new commandment, but an old commandment which you had from the beginning. The old commandment is the word [doctrine, teaching] which you have heard.

The suggested outline of the Epistle makes a break at the beginning of this verse.

I. Fellowship with the Father
   A. The Condition of Righteousness   1:5–2:6
   B. The Condition of Love   2:7–17

Difficulty in the outline occurs because there is no mention of love here until verse 9; and section A has so many other ideas in it that one wonders whether *The Condition of Righteousness* is the proper title.

John is about to repeat to his addressees an old commandment, one they had from the beginning. This most likely means the beginning of the Christian era, for these individual addressees did not have this commandment from the beginning of time. The reference is to the time they heard it. What this old commandment is, John does not make explicit. It is the *logos* which they heard. So far as the wording of the text goes, the *logos* is all the apostolic teaching. Even if John makes it more specific and restricts it to brotherly love a few verses below, it is hard to understand why Stott (p. 92) says the commandment is not moral, but social. Stott must have a peculiar sense of morality. The fact that thievery and honesty are social does not prevent them from being a matter of morality. Is it only our duties toward God narrowly regarded, that are moral, and not also our duties toward our fellow men?

If we wish to see the exact sense of the verse, it would be better not only to extend our view beyond a narrow social view to the more inclusive moral view, but to take the term *logos* in its widest sense, namely, the preaching of the gospel as a whole. If it is not so taken, this verse makes a very awkward introduction for verse 9; whereas if the whole gospel is first envisaged, the selection of one item in the later verse is not such a stylistic and logical shock.

2:8.   Again a new commandment I write to you, which is true in him and in you, because the darkness is disappearing and the true light already appears.

There are a number of puzzling points in this verse, the first of which is the oldness and newness of the same commandment. The text mentions commandments, in the plural, in verses 3 and 4; but no one is greatest. Verse 5 has the wider term, *logos*. Now verses 7 and 8 say *commandment*, in the singular; but there is no imperative before verse 15. In fact, the commandment in verse 7 is identified as the *logos*. If the commandment were to love God and mankind, it would be as old as Deuteronomy and new in the sense of being always applicable. If the reference is to apostolic preaching, and this is a better suggestion, it is not so old, only a decade or two, but equally applicable in every age. If somehow Deuteronomy and the Gospels can be brought together, the old commandment takes on new and clearer meaning in Christ and his sacrifice. It must be related to Christ, for the next phrase is, "which is true in him and in you." The later idea of the darkness passing away supports this interpretation.

Now, what is true in him and in us? No commandment, no imperative sentence can be true, or false. Only declarative sentences can be true. Furthermore, the word *which* is neuter, and *commandment* is feminine. What, then, is the antecedent of *which?* On this grammatical principle the relative could not refer to *logos*, for *logos* is masculine.

Sometimes a seminary professor, or even president, betrays his ignorance of Greek. One such Arminian, in opposition to the clear Calvinism of Ephesians 2:8, argued from the platform that the neuter demonstrative could not refer to faith because faith is feminine. The seminary president's logic was equally bad; but let us attend to the grammar. Even in classical Greek, not to mention the looser Koine, not only may abstract feminine nouns have a neuter relative or demonstrative; even concrete feminines may (compare Allen §101; Goodwin §925).

The upshot of this tedious grammar is that the antecedent of the *which* can be any of three things: (1) the commandment, (2) the *logos,* or (3) both. This is all that a knowledge of Greek can furnish. The choice depends on the reader's evaluation of the sense. The present writer chooses the third possibility as the best. *Commandment* cannot be ruled out (even though no commandment is specified) because it is the nearest noun. *Logos* alone suffers because it is not the nearest noun, although the sense would be better, as the next comment will show. Therefore, both seems best.

The reason why *logos* must be included in the antecedent is the word *true.* As said above, a commandment alone cannot be true. But what can be meant by saying that the gospel is true in him and in us? A derivative meaning of the word *alēthes* is *genuine.* English preserves the sense in the phrase "tried and true." Heraclitus (500 B.C.) explained that the visible world was permeated by a *logos* that was true. One of the fragments that has survived can be translated either "this theory, though always true, men do not understand," or "this logos, though it always exists," etc. We may, therefore, suppose John to have meant that Jesus was a genuine example of the gospel, and that the truth of the gospel is exemplified in us as well. A man is genuine or true if what he says is true. He means to keep his promises. He is a "real" man (as if others were not even human beings?). Christ told the truth; so do we; and we practice what we preach. It is wrong to make a sharp separation between the truth of a proposition and a "real" man. The latter depends on the former. He tells the truth. This becomes more evident in the next phrase.

If we need not ask why the gospel was true in Jesus—though the answer will finally be the same—we must certainly ask why the gospel is true in us. Because—John gives the answer: the word of life is true in us because the darkness is passing away and the true light already appears.

What is the darkness that is passing away? Is it the darkness of paganism? Is it the heresy of Gnosticism as Stott (p. 94) and others suggest? Is it the usual sinful state of new converts? Or is it Jewish theology?

It certainly cannot be Gnosticism, even though some commentators claim to find such references in this Epistle. But Gnosticism was not passing away. If indeed it had begun, it was to become popular in the next two centuries. It was coming, not going. Nor could it be the heresy of Docetism. Docetism, which was not limited to Gnosticism, was also just beginning. The idea of passing away gives the impression of something of long standing.

Could it be Hellenistic religion? The apostles were indeed making inroads into Greco-Roman religion. But there were still two long centuries of persecution before paganism would retreat.

It seems better to understand John as referring to something Jewish. Within the range of Judaism there are two possibilities. First, there is the rabbinic theology of the Pharisees. When they tried to read Moses, they had a veil of darkness upon their heart. The early Christians were all Jews, and they all were more or less influenced by Pharisaism. This perverted interpretation of the Old Testament was passing away. True enough, Judaism continues to the present day; but it long ago ceased to influence the people of God. Now John must have had some such idea as this in mind. But there is a second consideration, and if the Epistle is dated about A.D. 80, this other consideration could easily have been the more prominent in John's mind. Despite the evil influence of Pharisaism, there were some truly pious Jews during the reign of Herod. But even the pure Judaism of a man like Simeon and a widow like Anna was not the clear light of the gospel. These people were still in the shadows. Shadows and darkness therefore indicate, not merely Pharisaism, but also the incomplete knowledge of the pious. With the new revelation, initiated by Christ, and proclaimed by the apostles, the darkness was passing away and the truth now shines forth.

So also converts from paganism would likewise step from the falsity of their religions into the truth of Christian theology. But it is doubtful that John had that in mind. Even in A.D. 80 the church at Ephesus must still have included a large number of Jews. Then, too, the Greek converts, for more than 20 years now, had been studying the Old Testament. Hence, the historical situation allows and even favors a reference to the change from the Mosaic ceremonies to the full doctrine of the incarnation and atonement.

2:9.   He who says he is in the light and hates his brother is in darkness to this moment.

It is well to note the verb *say* here. What a man says is not always true. Failure to note this obvious fact has led to problems in understanding the Epistle of James 2:14. The man there *says* he has faith, but his claim is false. So here in John, the man says he is in the light, but he is not.

This verse is the first indication that John had one specific command in mind. There may have been a hint of it in verse 8, if we remember Jesus' words about a new commandment. But the Epistle began with the widest generalities: the word of life, the message we have heard, walking in the light, and coming closer, his commandments. Now he singles out one of them. Why did he single out this one? Was there a great deal of personal friction or animosity in the congregations he was writing to? We do not know.

However, we know something about the situation today. First, there is the matter of hypocrisy. People often join churches for the wrong reasons. They make a verbal profession, which they regard as a meaningless formula. The session that admits them, even if it is a conscientious session, cannot discern hypocrisy on short acquaintance. But since this member really does not believe the truth, since his intellectual convictions are not Christian, his actual state of mind eventually shows itself. What a man really believes inevitably expresses itself in his conduct, regardless of what he said by the words of his lips. Perhaps this evidence is more clearly seen in his disregard for the brethren than in his breaking some other law. I knew a practicing atheist who would not manufacture slot machines for gambling houses. If he could make games of skill or chance simply to provide entertainment, very well; but gambling, no. There are practicing atheists who are reliable bankers or lawyers. In these specific fields they do not betray their atheism—though atheism gives them no good reason for being honest. But they never show love for the brethren. And maybe for this reason John singled out this commandment.

There is another and still more dangerous situation that faces the orthodox churches with respect to love. In the recent past Christian Science made a great ado about love; but it was not Christian love. Christian Science may no longer be aggressive; but something worse has sprung into action. Joseph Fletcher's love and his situation ethics destroys all the Ten Commandments. Love sanctifies adultery, theft, and murder. It is necessary therefore, especially in these days, to define love. The Scripture does so: Love is obedience to the law. An emotion called love can never be relied upon to point out what it is right to do. As even Fletcher admits, a bride's love for her husband gives her no instruction on how to bake a cherry pie. Emotional love is usually wrong. Therefore, we need the scriptural injunctions to discover what conduct love commands. Love is obedience to the Ten Commandments with their implications.

2:10.   He who loves his brother remains in the light and there is no scandal in him.

The comments on verse 9 spill over into verse 10. The two are complements of each other; and further comment would spill over into verse 11. All that need be noted is that the word *scandal* means "cause for offense."

2:11.   He who hates his brother is in darkness and walks in darkness, and he does not know where he is going, because the darkness has blinded his eyes.

This is in a sense the converse of the preceding. John might have said, He who hates his brother is a scandal in the church. He is a hypocrite; and many people use his presence in the church as an excuse for not attending. Perhaps we should answer the excuse by admitting its truth and adding that even so the church could tolerate another one.

But John says something more than the simple converse. He does not follow up on the cause of offense or cause of stumbling to others; instead he describes the plight of the one who hates. Ignorance, or, really, false opinions have blinded his mind. He cannot think clearly, and hence he does not realize in what direction he is going.

Once three of us were hiking over a mountain. We planned, when we got to the top, to turn left and descend to a point some miles north of our start. I turned left at about 45 degrees, but could find no trail. The trouble was that I did not know in what direction I was going. I had the wrong conception of the necessary angle. Fortunately, one of the other two knew that the angle was more like 15 than 45 degrees. He found the trail and we descended.

The emphasis in this verse is not so much the idea that the hypocrite causes others to stumble, as it is that he is an offense to himself. When he thinks he can cheat a brother in some deal, he may indeed injure his brother and bring opprobrium upon the church. But what John says explicitly is that he injures himself. He is headed in the wrong direction and doesn't know it. The emphasis is considerable: *darkness* is mentioned three times. The good brother may indeed be injured; but he who hates the good brother is in darkness, walks in darkness, and is blinded by darkness. He is without the light of God's truth; and to use, or misuse, a phrase from Jude, he is heading toward "the blackness of darkness forever."

1:12. I write to you, children, because forgiven are your sins through his name.

The Epistle's outline, earlier suggested, divides the paragraphs this way:

> The Condition of Love   2:7-17
> 1. Love is light   7-11
> 2. Parenthetical address   12-14
> 3. Love for God excludes love of the world   15-17

It is hard to produce a completely satisfactory outline for this Epistle; but on any scheme, verses 12-14 are parenthetical. They state certain reasons why John wrote to these people. A more inclusive purpose was given in 1:3, 4. Some Greek editions and the NIV print this section as if it were poetry. It does indeed have a literary style: three times "I write," and three times "I wrote"; the first three to children, fathers, and young men, the second three to another word for children, then fathers, and young men. The literary symmetry is obvious; but it is not poetry. *Paradise Lost* is poetry; the *Areopagitica* is not.

The exact intention of the author is difficult to ascertain. In the prologue it was clear; but how does forgiveness of sins become the reason for writing? Similarly, the reasons stated in verses 13 and 14 are not clear. Could these all be reduced to the plain, and tasteless expression, "I am writing to you because you are Christians?"

The two triads also need explanation. One commentator says that John distinguishes his parishioners into three groups according to their spiritual age: those very recently converted, those who were converted long before, and those between. Another commentator says that the first of each triad addresses all Christians, for all are John's converts. Then he distinguishes the older members from the younger. This latter interpretation has a modicum of plausibility, if "conquering the evil one" is the triumph of relatively young Christians, as opposed to the state of Christians of long standing, who conquered the evil one years earlier. Yet what he says in the first two parts of each triad applies to all Christians, young and old.

Lenski, however, refuses to take these divisions as those of spiritual age. He insists on chronological age. He argues that the spiritually immature are called *nepios; neaniskoi* means young in natural life (p. 419). He supposes that these teenagers have indeed conquered the evil one. But, we ask, must *teknia* and *paidia* apply to babies? Besides, in the second triad the "babies" are said to know the Father, and the fathers are said to know the pre-incarnate Christ. But neither of these characteristics depends on chronological age. Let it be noted that Leski, inconsistently, does not interpret *teknia* and *paidia* literally or chronologically. Though it does not remove all the difficulties, it seems best to understand these ages as calculated from the day of conversion.

Not much comment is needed on the sense of the causal clauses. Sin is forgiven through the name of Jesus, and through no other name. God is indeed merciful, but as the Shorter Catechism says, "Repentance unto life is a saving grace whereby a sinner out of . . . apprehension of the mercy of God in Christ," etc.

A housewife of my acquaintance had to call a plumber on one occasion. As he came up from the basement to leave, she thought she ought to witness to him a little. So she made some remark about his hopes of heaven. Not expecting such a topic, the plumber was momentarily flustered; but then replied, "Oh, yes, I trust the church will pull me through." But, then, the plumber was not Reformed or Presbyterian.

1:13.   I am writing to you, fathers, because you know him [who was] from the beginning. I am writing to you, young men, because you have conquered the evil one.

Him who was or is from the beginning is, of course, the Lord Jesus Christ. The Epistle began with this concept. Now, while indeed the older Christians know this, one might suppose that relatively young Christians know this, too. But they are characterized as having conquered Satan. Does this suggest that even Christians of a few years standing do not know enough to preach the gospel and rule the church? Paul forbids recent converts to take prominent positions in the congregations. Even Timothy, to whose youth Paul referred, was a lifelong Christian, and chronologically about forty at the time. But Paul's instructions are not found in this verse.

1:14.   I wrote to you, children, because you know the Father. I wrote to you, fathers, because you know him [who was or is] from the beginning. I wrote to you, young men, because you are strong and the word of God remains in you and you have conquered the evil one.

Is there any difference between the reason given for writing to the children and that for the fathers? Westcott makes an ingenious suggestion.

> The sense of an immediate personal relationship to God (comp. John xiv.7) gives stability to all the gradations of human authority. In this respect "knowing the Father" is different from "knowing him that is from the beginning." The former involves a direct spiritual connexion; the latter involves besides an intellectual apprehension of the divine "plan." The knowledge "of the Father" is that of present love and submission: the knowledge of him "that is from the beginning" is sympathy with the Divine Thought which is fulfilled in all time. (p. 61)

This is highly imaginative. Could not one equally well say that knowledge of the Son is present love and submission, while knowledge of the Father has to do with the divine decree which is fulfilled in all time? Or, for that matter, why may not knowledge of the Father be an understanding of the [material in the] Westminster Confession, chapter 2, sections 1 and 2, while knowledge of the Son is an understanding of the creed of Chalcedon? This seems to be a better suggestion than Westcott's. But the text says neither. Further, why should spiritual or chronological children know the Father, and only come to know the Son in old age? Yet this is F. F. Bruce's view (p. 58).

Let the words suggest or stimulate whatever bright ideas one may think of; but we must remember that these ideas are not in the text.

The closest the reader can come to a degree of precision is to see that the strong young men (whether spiritual or chronological) have conquered the evil one. Even this is puzzling. It cannot mean that they have attained perfect sinlessness. And if the victory is only partially complete, even the children have had a partial victory, and the fathers should have achieved a greater victory than that of the strong young men. Similarly, it is encouraging to know that the word or teaching of God remains in their minds; but do not the fathers have a wider grasp of theology? Even the spiritually immature, along with their aberrations, have some theological truth and this word, minimum though it be, remains with them throughout life. Learning more does not cancel out the primary lessons. The greatest mathematician still has to use the multiplication table. The apostle Paul also enforces this lesson: "Let the teaching of Christ dwell in you richly in all wisdom" (Col. 3:16).

2:15.   Do not love the world nor the things in the world. If anyone love the world, the love of the Father is not in him.

The "world" here means unregenerate civilization. Pagan Rome and Greece loved athletics and sexual debauchery. The people crowded the stadiums and staged nudist parties. As John will say in 5:19, we know that all America lies in the grip of the devil. Some preachers proclaim that America is materialistic. So far as philosophy goes, there are no longer any materialists at all. If by "materialistic" these preachers mean greedy and money-mad, they may have some reason for saying so. But most "money-mad" people seek money in order to buy the pleasures of wine, women, and perhaps a little song. On the shirt of a hang-glider there was an inscription: Only one thing is better than hang-gliding. Under which inscription was the picture of a naked girl. And this was worn in public.

There are, of course, some few people who have other affections. Painters and musicians may praise art for art's sake. Utrillo and his mother were no doubt licentious drunks, but they really loved art. Some practicing atheists love politics. Perhaps they dream of Stalin and Idi Amin, for a fair number of people love power just for the fun of pushing people around. They delight in multiplying regulations for the citizenry. All this is the world that a Christian should not love. It is incompatible with a love for the Father.

It may be worth noting that the verb and noun here are forms of *agapaō*. Some recent theologians have elevated this verb and this love above *phileō* and far above *eros* and *eraō*. *Agapē* is supposed to be a very spiritual and special love for God; *phileō* is a love of friendship; and *eros* is sexual. But note that *eraō* in Homer is applied both to god and man in the same sentence. The object of *eraō* can also be a thing. In the New Testament *phileō* and *agapaō* are indistinguishable in meaning. But worst of all for these agapist theologians, in the Septuagint, in II Samuel 13:1ff., Amnon *ēgapēsen* Tamar; then later his hatred of her was greater than his *agapēn* had been. Here *agapē* designates incestuous love. The verb and noun simply mean *love*. What sort of love it is depends on the context. Even in the present verse, the object of *agapaō* is both the world (though negative) and the Father.

2:16. Because everything in the world, fleshly desire, the desire of the eyes, and the arrogance of life are not of the Father but of the world.

The reason the man of the previous verse has no love for the Father, is, if it be necessary to say so, that the main interests of such people have no divine or eternal value. No real present value, either. John summarizes these objects of fleshly desire under three categories: the desire of the flesh, the desire [both times, singular] of the eyes, and the boasting or arrogance of life. What concretely do these three phrases designate?

The desire of the flesh no doubt includes the promiscuous copulation of college students, and their wife-swapping later on. Yet this may not be uppermost in John's mind. The phrase may be inclusive of nearly all sinful desires, for the term *flesh* is the designation of the whole corrupt nature of man. Calvin says, "Paul when forbidding, in Romans 13:14, to make provision for the flesh as to its lusts, seems to me to be the best interpreter of this place. What, then, is the flesh there? Even the body and all that belongs to it . . . when worldly men, seeking to live softly and delicately, are intent only on their own advantages."

John Cotton (p. 178) also says much the same thing. He lists meat and drink (though gluttony does not now seem to be a prevalent sin), pastimes, and pleasures. A. W. Pink mentions the pastimes and pleasures of the dance and gambling. He also points out that otherwise legitimate objects of desire become sinful when pushed to excess and to the exclusion of religious duties. He further suggests that the desire of the eyes is not so much looking at a woman to lust after her as it is the covetousness and malice engendered by seeing the success and fortune of another person. The arrogance or boastfulness of life, Lenski identifies with the conviction that one can direct his course of life without considering God's laws. This would include not only Hitler and Stalin, but also many American bureaucrats whose chief delight is to control other people.

Most of the commentators take pains to notice that many objects of desire are good and pleasing to God. They become sinful either by reason of excessive desire for them, or by total disregard for God. In these days this is particularly true in the sphere of economics. Some labor unions are controlled by the Mafia. The previous two presidents of the Teamsters Union—no insignificant organization—were convicted criminals; and the Union's present president bids fair to become one. It is also true that some financiers are guilty of embezzlement. Congressmen, apparently with impunity, have accepted bribes, while the nation, or at least the press, clamors against those who paid the bribes. The Supreme Court has legalized the murder of innocent babies and virtually abolished the death penalty for murder. Nevertheless, this does not mean that the institution of government, of business, or of labor unions is intrinsically evil. On the other hand, it is also true that many governmental programs to help the poor are not necessarily good. The Third World, as it is now called, that is, the developing nations clamor for aid from the richer nations; and liberals in the richer nations frequently propose programs that would impoverish the rich. This is a mistake into which many religious people have fallen. F. F. Bruce (p. 61) says,

If, in a world where the richer nations tend to become richer and the poorer to become poorer, the administration of a richer nation makes further increases in economic prosperity a major plank in its platform, the Christian—especially the Christian who prefers to remain as detached as possible from political responsibility—must be constantly vigilant lest his own life reflect the unadmitted assumptions underlying such a policy.

But it is F. F. Bruce's underlying assumptions that a Christian should reject. Apparently tinged by Marxism, Bruce seems to think that there is a fixed quantity of wealth in the world, and if one nation gets richer another must get poorer. This is not the case, for several reasons. China and India have had as much and more natural resources than France, Germany, and the United States combined. But their political and religious systems have prevented them from developing. India under the British Empire and Russia under the Czars had enough food and actually could export large quantities. Changes in government brought both, the one to a point of starvation, the other to the importing of huge surpluses of capitalist wheat. Then, too, the wealth of the West has grown by industrialization and invention. The United States did not become richer by making poor nations poorer. It became rich by the invention of the cotton gin, the linotype machine, and television. We can become richer still, if government can be kept in bounds, by the utilization of solar energy. Does Bruce think that our success in solar heating will make the poor nations poorer? Finally, not to extend this political and economic argument beyond reason, the falling dollar and our inflation not only make us poorer—and so on Bruce's view should make Ethiopia and Zambia richer—but sends shivers of poverty throughout the world. We have caught a bad cold, and the other nations got pneumonia. If we get poorer, by reason of our governmental extravagance, the whole world will starve. The economic fact is that all nations get rich together or get poor together. If now, anyone should be inclined to dislike a paragraph on economics in a commentary on John, let him remember that a commentary should not use the Epistle as a defense for socialism.

2:17.   The world, however, and its desire, is passing away; but he who does the will of God remains forever.

Translation: the last verb can be translated abides, remains, endures, continues.

Worldly aims and ambitions not only will be swept away when the Lord returns; even before death the wicked man is often convinced of the vanity, the uselessness of his life. He is forced to admit he "cannot take it with him." At a still earlier age the athlete is a victim of drugs, torn ligaments, and broken bones. The rake is impotent; the party-goer, an alcoholic. But those who live a calm, unemotional, steady Christian life have a sense of satisfaction. What is more, they will remain satisfied in heaven forever.

This steadiness characterizes the man who does the will of God. Here again we see the "legalism" that antinomians despise. In this regard, it may be noted that law and obedience are more indicated by the phrase, the will of God, than they would have been by the phrase, the will of the Father. The term *Father* has a family and soteric connotation, while the word *God* may suggest the Lawgiver. Of course, here the *will* of God designates his preceptive, not his decretive, will, since no one violates the latter.

The outline of the Epistle has now gone like this, and continues:

B. The Condition of Love
   1. Love is light   2:7-11
   2. Parenthesis   2:12-14
   3. Love of God excludes love of the world   2:15-17
C. The Condition of Belief   2:18-28
   1. Heresy destroys fellowship   2:18-22
   2. Exhortation   2:23-28

2:18.   Children, it is the last hour, and as you heard that antichrist is coming, even now many antichrists have arisen; for which reason we know that it is the last hour.

Translation: Since no definite article precedes the word *hour*, it is possible to translate the phrase as "a last hour." It might refer to a last chance these people had. But Greek articles are puzzling. The grammars and learned articles go on at great length. Here we only say that in English the article can be inserted or left out. So much for the translation.

The interpretation is more difficult than the Greek grammar. Obviously in this twentieth century we cannot believe that the Spirit of God, who controlled John's words, meant that the Second Advent would occur in the next 60 minutes.

It was Westcott who suggested "a"—indefinite article—last hour; by which he means "the general character of the period and not its specific relation to 'the end.' It was a period of critical change, 'a last hour,' but not definitely 'the last hour.' " Westcott also gives references, some in the Old Testament, many in the New, to similar phraseology.

Lenski supports the same translation with some grammatical comments, plus the observation that " 'Last hour' appears only here in this verse and is not used otherwise." This observation is more convincing than the grammatical remarks. He also notes—what is well-known—that the word *hour* hardly ever means 60 minutes. In the Gospel, 4:21, 23, *hour* refers to all the years from that day until Christ's return, and even afterward. The meaning is the same in John 5:25. In John 16:2, 25 (where the KJV translates *ōra* as *time*) and verse 26, the word *hour* and *day* refer to the same period of time.

A theological difficulty arises if the phrase is taken to mean "the last hour." Since history has now proceeded for 2000 years, "the last hour" would imply that John falsely prophesied that the Lord would return before A.D. 100.

Yet there is a difficulty in the idea of "a last time," or "an eschatological time," as if there would be later times of this sort. Verse 28 seems to suggest that this "hour" extends from John's day on to the Parousia. This receives support in I Corinthians 10:11, "upon whom [the people of Paul's day] the ends of the world are come." Thus, the gospel age is called the end time of the world, or the end of the ages. I Peter 4:7 contains a similar idea. Hebrews 9:26 puts Christ's crucifixion at the end or completion of the ages.

John Cotton makes some interesting remarks.

> Why do the Scriptures call them [John's days] the last days, since there have been fifteen centuries and more since then? I answer, the apostles did not mean that the last judgment was to come immediately, for . . . Paul seriously dissuaded them from expecting it so suddenly . . . there must first be an apostasy. . . . But why did they call them the last times? (1) Because they are the last period of time before the last judgment. (a) The first period was from Adam to Moses . . . (b) The second period of time was from Moses to Christ . . . (c) The third period . . . is from Christ's time to the end of the world. . . . If this gospel age is the last

time, then we may certainly conclude that not so much time shall pass from Christ to the end of the world as passed from Adam to Christ.

One might argue, on the other hand, that since the time from Adam to Christ was the preparation for a later age, the time between Christ's first and second advents is "certainly" much longer because one's preparation for his life's work is shorter than the rest of his life. However, most readers of this book are doubtless well aware of the futility of setting dates.

The next phrase is, "you have heard that antichrist is coming." Since the term occurs only five times in the New Testament, four times in this Epistle and once in the next, the fact that John's addressees were already familiar with the idea gives us a better understanding of what was preached in the first century. While Paul does not use the term, yet in II Thessalonians, a letter of early date, he mentions "the man of sin, the son of destruction." In this passage the definite article is used with the man of sin, the son of destruction, and the one who opposes God. The language seems to indicate a single individual.

John Cotton will not have it so (p. 219). He argues that the definite article is not always a sign of an individual person. In monarchies one may say the king made this law; yet it may not be the present king. Matthew 13:3 says the sower went forth to sow; but it does not refer to any definite farmer. And Cotton also argues that in II Thessalonians 2:3–8 the man of sin is at that time merely unrevealed; he will continue to operate through this age in a disguised fashion, and then he will be revealed and destroyed. If so, the man of sin cannot be an individual; no individual lives several thousand years. Therefore, the man of sin must be a continuing power of some sort. The Reformation martyrs and their sons knew the identity of that continuing power, but their great grandchildren have forgotten.

John, however, speaks of many antichrists then active. So does II Peter 2:1—"false prophets who introduce heresies of destruction."[3] Clearly, then, the apostles from the earliest years had been warning the infant church, not only against a future Antichrist, but against false prophets and heretical doctrine. The presence of these many heretics John takes as a sure indication that this is an eschatological hour, or one might better say an hour of danger.

---

[3]See my commentary on II Peter, *I and II Peter* (Jefferson, Maryland: The Trinity Foundation, 1980).

2:19.   They went out from us, but they were not of us; for if they had been of us, they would have remained with us. But in order that they might be clearly seen that they are not all of us.

The translation: The translations in this commentary do not aim at a style suitable to complete versions for public use. English has been twisted a little in order to preserve some of the Greek characteristics. Not all can be preserved. Here there is a play on words in that the word *from* (fourth word in the verse above) and the word *of* that occurs three times in the remainder of the verse are the same word *(ex)*. Anyone who has tried to translate jokes from one language to another recognizes the impossibilities. The second sentence of the translation is very literal in order to show its elliptical form. Translators regularly insert a phrase to complete the thought as: "But they went out in order that it might be shown" (NASB). Not only are words inserted but to improve the English the plural "they might be clearly seen" has been changed to the singular.

These antichrists originated in the church; they were members of the congregation. So, too, the final Antichrist will sit on a throne in the temple of God. The church of God has many external enemies. Idi Amin, like Nero, bludgeoned Christians to death. But the worst enemies are to be found in the church organization. Facing external oppression the church can remain pure. During the seven wars of religion in France the Huguenots preserved a strong and pure faith. Military victory corrupted their leader. So, too, in Scotland. The savage James II and bloody Claverhouse did not damage the Covenanter movement as much as the Christian king who ended the persecution and made himself the head of the Scottish church. Princeton Seminary and Fuller, as others, were corrupted from within.

John and the Asian churches seem to have enjoyed a less painful divine providence. In their case the heretical teachers left the church. It does not say they were excommunicated. Their exodus seems voluntary. Perhaps they were psychologically incapable of bearing up under strong orthodox teaching. Then they left, they deserted the apostles, and made it evident to all that their doctrine was not Christian.

Perhaps another word should have been mentioned as a matter of translation. But translation is sometimes more interpretation than grammar; and there are degrees of mixture. The conjunction after "that they might be clearly seen" is *oti*. It means either *that* or *because*. It seems to the present writer that what was made clear was *that* they were not true members of the body of Christ. Before their withdrawal many in the congregation presumably thought they were true, though perhaps confused, Christians. But now their exodus makes it clear that they were not. Lenski disagrees and translates *oti* as *because*. The antichrists were made evident because they left. This interpretation can be supported by insisting that "made evident" is plural. But the bare statement "they were made evident" is insufficient in the context. Of course, they evidently went out. But this made it evident to the Christians that the false prophets were not of us. At the end of the preceding verse it is clear that John wants his people to know something. This something is the existence of antichrists as signs of an hour of danger. Hence, the people are to know *that* Cerinthus (perhaps) was a false prophet. No doubt Cerinthus went out because he was not a Christian; but John wants his little children, young men, and fathers to know *that* the heretics were heretics.

There is another point at which translation and interpretation meet. The word is *ina*. In classical Greek *ina* is always purposive. In Koinē it may introduce either a purpose or a result clause. Then how should we read it? They went out in order that their true nature should be known; or, they went out with the result that their true nature became evident? Now rather obviously it was not the purpose of the antichrists to make known their anti-Christian character. This was the result. Yet the emphatic position of *ina*, with the strong adversative *alla*, inclines one to preserve, if possible, the original purposive meaning of the conjunction. This is possible and after consideration the reader may think it preferable. John was not so much concerned with a mere historical sequence. He is interested in church history in the light of divine providence. There will be a final Antichrist; there are many antichrists now. Such is God's plan. Therefore, God determined their exodus in order to make their falsity evident to the true believers. "In order that their true nature should be made evident" is God's purpose.

2:20.   And you have an anointing from the holy [Spirit] and you all know.

Textual note: The majority of manuscripts read, "You know all things." A few have, "You all know." The latter should be adopted only if the former does not make good sense. One ancient version says, "You know all people." Metzger's *Textual Commentary*, assuming "the claims of a few to possess esoteric knowledge" prefers, "You all know." Then they gratuitously explain, "The reading *panta* . . . was regarded as a correction introduced by copyists who felt the need of an object after *oidamen*." There is no evidence for this supposition. We may equally well suppose that John wrote, "You know all things," for *oidamen* certainly seems to need an object; and then a careless copyist, not for any doctrinal reason, or literary reason either, but just by accident, wrote *pantes*.

The word *chrisma* does not mean the act of anointing. If it did, the verb would have been an aorist: you had the anointing. The verb is present, you have an "anointment." The noun refers to the blessing conferred, not to the conferral. We may, however, ask what was conferred, how, and when? Some commentators take the conferring as baptism; and Westcott refers to Acts 8:18, where the scales fell from Paul's eyes. But it is to be noted that baptism did not produce this result. The scales fell *before* Paul was baptized. Besides which, Paul's conversion and blindness, and Ananias' opening of Paul's eyes, are miraculous and not normative for all Christians. Hence, we cannot follow Westcott when he says, "This gift is referred to a definite time (v. 27); and the narrative of the Acts fixes this normally at the imposition of hands which *followed* on Baptism." Then for evangelical reasons too long to detail, we reject the sacramentarianism on which such theories are based.

If any content is to be attributed to this anointing, an enduring gift that follows the act, its nature must be discovered in the next phrase: "you all know." Knowledge, then, is the gift or *chrisma*. Perhaps "you know all things." Verse 27 says so, whether verse 20 does or not. The emphasis is on knowledge.

F.F. Bruce, defending "you all know," that there was an elite who claimed great knowledge, and that John comforted his people by saying they all had knowledge, too. But the contrast is not in the text. The picture of the heretics is not that of those who have or claim to have great knowledge as opposed to the humble ignorant people in the pews. The contrast is between those who deny that Christ came in the flesh and the orthodox doctrine of the incarnation. On this ground we may interpret the phrase as "you all know the doctrine of the incarnation, and hence you all can identify these false prophets." The following verses support this interpretation.

> **2:21.   I did not write to you because you do not know the truth, but because you know it, and because every lie is not of the truth.**

Translation: The second half of the verse can be properly translated "because you know it and (also) that every lie is not of the truth."

The very obvious emphasis on knowledge—which one would hardly expect in an argument against Gnosticism—supports the idea that the anointing was an impartation of doctrinal teaching. Westcott uses the words of verse 27, "which you received" to sustain his sacramentarian notion of an instantaneous blessing conferred by baptism. But the aorist can as well refer to a program of apostolic teaching. In fact, the imperfect tense would be quite puzzling. These people had heard the gospel for 20 years or more, and they *received* it.

Hence, in the verse at hand, John wrote because they knew the truth. If it be said that this would be a reason for not writing, two replies can be made. First, he could write to remind them of what they knew. He did not have to repeat the doctrine, but he brought it to their attention. Second, although they knew the doctrine, they might have been slow in seeing how it applied to Cerinthus, or whomever it might be. And third, since there were children and young men, as well as fathers, these of recent standing needed the admonition more than the mature Christians did.

This last point suggests another consideration. The apostles never wrote to people who did not know. Their letters were never intended to convert anybody. Every Epistle, and Luke 1:1-4 suggests every Gospel as well, was written to Christians. They could and should use the scriptural material in their proclamation to the pagans; but the Scriptures are first of all addressed to those already converted.

In contrast with knowledge and truth, John makes the obvious remark that no lie is of the truth. The apostle's emphasis on knowledge and truth, along with his condemnation of lies or false doctrine, is not welcome to American religious life in the second half of the twentieth century. In 1967 the United Presbyterian Church in the U.S.A. not only put the Westminster Confession on the shelf, but, worse, changed the ordination vows so that an ordinand would not subscribe to any doctrine. It is doubtful if the new vows require even a vague belief in God. So-called evangelicals are not too much better. Emphasis is placed on emotional experiences, perhaps including unknown tongues, and doctrine is denounced as "cold intellectualism." If the Psalms are singled out as conspicuously emotional, it should be noted that they contain at least 40 references to truth, not to mention the 176 verses of Psalm 119. And is not Genesis truth? In the New Testament John in particular stresses truth. His Gospel is full of doctrine. False doctrine is a lie; it is the opposite of truth; and no amount of putative devotional experience can substitute for it.

> **2:22.   Who is the liar, if not the one who denies that Jesus is the Messiah? He is the antichrist, he who denies the Father and the Son.**

The translation: Actually the Greek says, "Who is the liar, if not the one who denies that Jesus is not the Christ." In English double negatives make a positive; but in Greek the multiplication of negatives increases the negative force. Hebrews has a verse with five negatives; it was well approximated in the hymn,

> The soul that on Jesus has leaned for repose,
> I'll never, no never, desert to his foes.
> That soul though all hell should endeavor to shake,
> I'll never, no never, no never forsake.

As for the Greek article, previously mentioned, we note that the text says "the liar," not a liar. And in the middle of the verse it says, "This one is the antichrist," not an antichrist. Clearly neither of these definite articles indicates a single individual person. The article here emphasizes a characteristic. Anyone who denies that Jesus has come in the flesh is controlled by the prince of lies.

The title in the phrase "who denies that Jesus is the Messiah" is really a poor, though accurate, translation because the term Messiah has become ambiguous. If given its correct Old Testament meaning, the assertion stands. But many Jews, before and after Jesus' earthly ministry, did not believe that the Messiah would be God incarnate.

Messiah in Hebrew and *Christos* in Greek mean the Anointed One. But kings and priests were anointed. It is better, therefore, to translate or transliterate the phrase as "Jesus is the Christ." The word *Christ,* because of the Nicene and Chalcedonian creeds, is not so vague: it has been firmly determined to mean the Second Person of the Trinity, the only Son of God.

Now, very obviously, there cannot be a Second Person, unless there is a First. Therefore, John adds: "he who denies the Father and the Son." And at this point the next verse must be brought into view in order to understand this one. Remember there are no verse divisions in the manuscripts. If you write, even a long letter to a friend, you do not divide your script into verses, though you may use paragraphs. There is a story that the verses were introduced by a monk who was reading the Bible while riding on his mule. He had a pen in his hand, and every time the mule jerked, his pen hit the manuscript and made a verse division. The actual process of division, presumably by Stephanus (Etienne) at the time of the Reformation, was no less illogical. A mule could have done as well (almost).

2:23.   Everyone who denies the Son does not have the Father, either. He who confesses the Son has the Father also.

Textual note: The Textus Receptus, that is the text of Erasmus published by Stephanus, from which the King James version was translated, does not have the last sentence of this verse; and the King James version prints it in italics, which is the sign that the words do not occur in the Greek manuscripts. Strange to say, there is no doubt that the sentence is genuine and original. Modern critical texts do not list its omission in any manuscript. Frequently modern critical editions delete words and phrases as pleases their subjective assumptions. But here is one place where the Textus Receptus is guilty. Now, back to the commentary.

John tells us, and tells the world, that a bare theism, such as Unitarians and Moslems profess, is not theism at all. The only God is a Trinity. If in particular one does not believe in Jesus Christ, he does not have God at all. For there is only one God and he is the Father of our Lord Christ. Without the Son, there is no Father. A man cannot have either one without the other also.

If the aim of commentaries is to explain what the words mean, they may be permitted also to clarify the meaning by contemporary examples and applications. In the present decades the American public has been concerned or disturbed with references to prayers in the public schools and at government functions, such as the sessions of Congress. Now, the present writer has no animosity against prayer, anywhere or at any time; but it must be prayer to the only God. The State of New York, if I am correct, through the civil Board of Education, composed and imposed a prayer to be said in the public schools. But as a good Christian might expect, it was not a prayer that a good Christian could make, for it was not addressed to God. God can be addressed only through his only Son. A prayer that satisfies "everybody" is just the prayer that no Christian should offer. Islam, Hinduism, the present Jewish religion, and Christianity have nothing in common. They may all use the word *God,* but the Christian will not admit that Shiva or Allah is God. God is the Father of Jesus Christ. There is none other.[4]

The particular heresy that distressed the apostle was not so much Gnosticism as Docetism. Such is the inference that may be drawn from 4:2–3 when we come to them. It was a denial that the Son of God had come in the flesh. This Docetism is a part of Gnosticism, but not all Docetism is Gnostic. The view was that Jesus was born a very ordinary person. Then at his baptism the divine Logos came down and dwelt in him. Finally, just before he died on the cross, the Logos reascended, upon which loss the man Jesus cried out, "My God, my God, why hast thou forsaken me?"

This original Docetism is not widespread today; but echoes and similarities sometimes occur. A prominent evangelist, just a few years ago, preaching in Africa, asserted that Jesus is God in a body. Probably he did not hold that God deserted him on the cross. But at any rate he replaced Jesus' "reasonable soul" (as the Westminster standards call it) with God, or the Logos, or the Holy Spirit. This is implicitly a denial of the incarnation, for the baby Jesus, on this view, was not a

---

[4]On the exclusiveness of Christianity and the absence of any common belief among the religions, see my *Religion, Reason and Revelation,* chapter 1.

full human nature. Zinzendorf also, praised so greatly for his piety, was not a Trinitarian, for he held that Christ was the only divine Person, the Father appearing as a Son. Zinzendorf claimed to be a Lutheran and a successor to the Hussites and Moravians. He was undoubtedly a leader of Pietism. This movement was largely uninterested in doctrine, but even so no one can abolish all teaching and remain rational. Zinzendorf's doctrine of the incarnation does not meet John's standards, even if it is not quite the same as that of Cerinthus.

It is to be noted that while John strongly condemns all those who do not love the brethren, namely, those who hate and walk in darkness, the ultimate condemnation, the stigma of the Antichrist, is imposed on those whose theology is heretical. Their thoughts are worse than their actions. Indeed, it is the thoughts that control the actions. The apostle, in his Gospel 8:44 and context, quotes Jesus to the same effect. In the same chapter, verse 51, Jesus asserts the converse: "If anyone maintains my doctrine, he shall not see death, ever."

The Epistle also gives its converse: "He who confesses the Son has the Father also." This reminds us of Romans 10:9-10 where Paul writes, "If thou shalt confess with thy mouth that Jesus is Lord, and believe in thine heart that God hath raised him from the dead, thou shalt be saved." Now, the Old Testament frequently contrasts what people say with their mouths, with what they believe in their hearts. But it rather seems that the word *confess* is stronger than the word *say.* The idea of confession includes the idea of sincerity. Furthermore, the term suggests, and this is what both Paul and John must have meant, a public confession. It is necessary to believe in the heart, but God also requires us to make this belief known publicly. Christians should not seek martyrdom deliberately; indeed they should avoid it by all moral means. Nevertheless, we must confess publicly, and we in America should lament the fate of our brethren in communist countries. I hope I never have to suffer as they have; and I wonder if I could equal their constancy.

2:24.   Let what you have heard from the beginning remain in you; if what you have heard from the beginning remains in you, you also shall remain in the Son and in the Father.

In the first place this exhortation indicates that the doctrine of the incarnation, as well as the propitiation, was taught to the new converts. Theology is not to be reserved until converts become mature. It is theology that matures them, and this instruction must begin from the beginning. To this instruction the converts must pay attention and take care not to forget. What they heard must remain with them. They should think about it, talk about it, and even sing about it.

> We praise thee, O God;
> We acknowledge thee to be the Lord
> . . .
> Heaven and earth are full of the majesty of thy Glory.
> . . .
> Thine adorable, true, and only Son
> . . .
> Thou art the King of Glory, O Christ
> . . .
> Thou didst humble Thyself to be born of a Virgin
> . . .
> We believe that Thou shalt come to be our Judge.

Too many congregations today sing that grand old hymn of the church:

> Climb, climb up sunshine mountain
> Faces all aglow.

But Christianity is theocentric, not egocentric.

2:25.   And this is the promise which he himself promised to us, eternal life.

What is this promise, and what is eternal life? If these two terms include some elements not mentioned explicitly in the preceding verses, they surely include what has been mentioned. Commentators frequently say that the promise is the gospel. So it is. But what is the gospel—the good news? A most important part of the news—in the headlines, not buried two-thirds of the way down the column—is the information that Christ has come in the flesh. The doctrine of the Trinity is good news. Most assuredly the good news includes Christ's propitiation of the Father. This was said earlier (2:2); by no means is it excluded here. The promise is the whole gospel: the main points and the subsidiary points as well. What, then, is life eternal, the life of the ages, the resurrection life, the life to come, which nonetheless we begin to have now? Jesus in his High Priestly prayer said, "This is life eternal, that they should know Thee, the only true God, and Jesus Christ, whom Thou hast sent" (John 17:3). If any verse defines eternal life, this is it. Eternal life is knowledge of the Father and the Son. Just because the *Gnostics* (those who *know*) were heretics is no good reason for deprecating knowledge. The trouble with the Gnostics was that they did not *know*. They had opinions, beliefs, theories, theology; but their views were false; their theology was error, not knowledge. As it is wrong to reject *faith* or *belief,* just because various people believe falsehoods, so it is wrong to belittle knowledge and theology. Yet this sort of pietism is, in various degrees, the chief weakness of present day conservative Christians. It behooves us to retain what we have heard from the beginning, to continue stedfastly in the apostles' doctrine, to have the mind of Christ, for what eye hath not seen, nor ear heard, God has revealed to us, and we have received the Spirit so that we might know the things of God.

2:26.   These things I wrote to you about those who are deceiving you.

The translation: "Deceiving" is good enough. The KJV "seducing" is so also. Better perhaps is the phrase "cause to wander." The Greek astronomers called the planets *planets,* because, in contrast with the stars, the planets *wandered.* Hence the verb means to lead astray, deceive, or delude. It is not translation, but interpretation, a good interpretation, to make it read "those who are trying to deceive you." The verse, so short, merely states the reason, or one reason, that John wrote his letter.

2:27.   And you, the anointing which you received from him remains in you; and you do not need anyone to teach you. But as his anointing teaches you about everything, and it is true and is not false, and as it taught you, remain in it.

The translation: A literal translation here makes awkward English. It is rather awkward Greek, too. The last word of the verse presents a difficulty. The pronoun is either masculine or neuter: the two genders have the same form. All the English versions translate it as masculine: "remain in him." But the only antecedent *noun* is the anointing (neuter); it is this noun that controls the phrase, "is true and is not false." The subject of the verb *teach* is the neuter term *anointing*. Then how can the final *autō* be anything or anyone else? It makes little difference whether the last verb, *remain,* is indicative or imperative.

In verse 20 we concluded that the anointing was not baptism. The present verse supports the identification of the anointing as the gospel. This is what they received. It is a teaching. For this reason John's addressees do not need anyone [else] to teach them. Of course, they need teaching. Is not John teaching them all through this letter? The meaning must be that they do not need any further teaching to recognize that the heretics in view are heretics. The verse applies to this limited situation. Evangelical Christians must strenuously resist the mystical claim that the Holy Spirit apart from the Scripture gives us all we need. A minister of my acquaintance, when I quoted Romans 10:9-10, ejaculated, "Oh, no; not that way. The Holy Spirit gives us the ability to discern the state of a man's heart, and we receive him into membership because the Holy Spirit tells us he is regenerate." Unfortunately this young minister took to himself a paramour, divorced his wife, and married his girlfriend, splitting his congregation.

That the *anointment* is the gospel is clear from its being called *true* and not false. This applies to Romans 10:9-10. Admittedly, we sometimes talk of false disciples and true disciples; we can say that the Holy Spirit is *true,* but it is awkward to say that he is not a lie, or not false. The wording of the verse scarcely allows any other interpretation. The anointing is the teaching. The simple, literal meaning of true and false attaches to propositions, and these have been identified as the doctrine of the Incarnation. So far as this unmasks the Docetists, no further teaching is necessary.

How, then, does the "unction" teach us about all things? The previous sentence is one possible answer. It limits all things to the subjects under discussion. Or one could imagine that the teaching actually given on the incarnation presupposes or implies all other scriptural teaching. Since God is rational, and not insane, truth forms a completely logical system. As geometry cannot exist without theorem 17, that is, one cannot establish theorems 2 and 20 without theorem 17, so, too, there is no incarnation without sanctification, and no Trinity without the priesthood of all believers. Therefore, as you have been taught, stick with it!

2:28.   And now, children, remain in him, in order that, if he should appear, we may have confidence and not be ashamed from him in his presence.

The translation: Three points must be noted. First, the pronouns at the end of the verse are clearly masculine because the phrase refers to the return of Christ. Therefore, the *autō* at the beginning of the verse is probably masculine also. Certainly, it does not have to refer to the neuter message of the previous verse. These masculine pronouns have induced most commentators to suppose that the pronouns in the previous verse are masculine as well. However, this does not follow. If verses 28 and 29 form a new paragraph, as they are printed in many editions, nothing prevents a change from neuter to masculine. One could even translate this verse as, "Remain in it, so that if he should appear. . . ." This is grammatically quite possible, and more plausible than at first it might appear.

Second, the phrases "if he should appear," "if he should be revealed" (passive), or "when he shall appear" as the King James version has it, are equally correct. The Greek verb is passive; but the King James makes the best sense in English. Third, *parousia* does not mean *coming* or *advent;* it means *presence.*

If we remain in him, and that means to maintain his truth, we shall have confidence when he returns. The word *if (ean)* does not cast any doubt on the certainty of his coming again. Blass-Debrunner (371-4) says, *"Ean* with the subjunctive denotes that which under certain circumstances is expected."

By remaining in Christ we shall have confidence in his presence. Others will have no confidence and will call to the rocks and the mountains to fall on them and hide them from the wrath of the Lamb. But we shall not be ashamed from him. The phrase is peculiar. It does not mean so much to be ashamed before him, as to shrink or slink away from him in shame, as the NASB puts it.

2:29. **If you know that he is just, you know also that everyone who does justly has been born of him.**

There are here two different verbs for "know": *eidēte* and *ginōskete*. Westcott, who surely knew plenty of Greek, wrote, "Knowledge which is absolute *(eidēte)* becomes the basis of knowledge which is realized in observation *(ginōskete)*." Stott, though his terminology is different, says virtually the opposite: "If you know as a fact *(eidēte)* [and facts are known by observation] that God is righteous, John says, then you will perceive as a logical consequence *(ginōskete)* [and are not logical consequences absolute?] that everyone that doeth righteousness is born of him."[5]

Westcott, to support his view, refers to John 2:24; but this hardly favors his contention, for Christ's knowledge in that verse was "absolute," and not an inference from limited observation. It says he knew *(ginōskein)* all men. Even if this means only all who were in Jerusalem at the feast, it is not likely that he had observed every individual there. Rather, he knew that the heart of man is deceitful above measure, and that they would later reject and crucify him; from this scriptural principle and his divine foreknowledge he deduced that he should not trust these people. Similarly, if we know that Christ is just or righteous, we infer, with the help of some unexpressed premises such as that only the power of God can make a man act righteously,—we infer that anyone who does righteously has been born of God.

Oida, eidenai, in I Corinthians 1:16 and I Thessalonians 5:12 could more easily be classified as observational than as absolute. Matthew 26:70 has the same verb; it does not refer to some eternal principle; it is unmistakably bound to its immediate present. Two passages from Mark are also pertinent. Mark 2:10 tells us about the paralytic whose friends let him down through the roof. Jesus said, "Thy sins be forgiven thee." The scribes took offense. Jesus answered them: "But that ye may know *(eidēte)*. . . ." The scribes were about to get this knowledge by observing the man get up and walk out carrying his

---

[5]Nigel Turner, *Grammatical Insights,* pp. 152ff., favors Stott's view more than Westcott's, though there can hardly have been any influence from one on the other, since Stott's book was published in 1964 and Turner's in 1965. Turner gives many details, but his conclusion is confused.

bed. By Westcott's criterion the verb would have had to be *ginōskō*.
Mark 4:13 is similar. Jesus said: "You do not *oidate* this parable, and
how will you *gnōsesthe* all parables." Now, it might seem that a single
parable could qualify for knowledge by observation, by hearing it
told; and if that be true, the verb should have been *ginōskō* instead of
oida. But a knowledge of all parables is surely more absolute than
observational. So the verb should have been *oida* instead of *ginōskō*.
Of course, the whole argument is confused because the term *absolute*
is so vague. Once again, *oida* is the perfect of a defunct verb *to see*. It
means I have seen, that is, I know. But since it is perfect in form, one
must use the perfect of another verb to say *I have known*. This other
verb is *ginōskō*. I am afraid that the very learned Westcott is a little
pedantic. No doubt the reader will reply that I can be more than a little
pedantic without being learned. My conclusion, however, is easily
understood: the two verbs mean the same thing.

But now having taken a little fling at Westcott, we may commend
him on his interpretation of the last pronoun in the verse, "we have
been born of *him*." Does this *him* refer to God the Father or to Jesus
Christ? Christians are called sons of God, but never sons of Christ. Yet
the pronoun *autou* surely refers to Christ. On this Westcott says,

> The true solution to the difficulty seems to be that when St. John thinks
> of God in relation to men he never thinks of him apart from Christ
> (comp. c. v. 20). And again he never thinks of Christ in his human
> nature without adding the thought of his divine nature. Thus a rapid
> transition is possible from the one aspect of the Lord's divine-human
> Person to the other. Here the passage is from Christ to God . . . and
> conversely in iii. 1–4 the passage is from God to Christ . . . yet without
> any change of Person.

So ends chapter 2.

The Third Chapter

THE more one tries to fit the verses and paragraphs into the outline earlier suggested, the less one likes the outline. It had

II. Our Sonship
    B. Sonship Tested by Righteousness   2:29–3:10a
        1. Righteousness, a sign of sonship   2:29
        2. Sonship causes righteousness (because sin is incompatible with abiding in him)   3:1–7
        3. Sin is of the Devil   3:8–10a

But other outlines make the main break at 2:26, and others at 3:1. For example, Westcott puts it this way:

B. The Conflict of Truth and Falsehood   2:18–46
    1. The revelation of Falsehood and Truth   2:18–29
    2. The children of God and the children of the devil   3:1–12
    3. etc.

Note that one outline brings a section to an end at 3:12, while another stopped at 3:10. If by now the reader is disgusted with commentaries, nothing could please the commentators more than his attempting to make a better outline.

> **3:1.**   **See what love the Father has given us in order that we may be called children of God. And we are. Therefore the world does not know us because it did not know him.**

The text: Why the Textus Receptus omitted the two words "and we are" is a mystery. The manuscript evidence is very strong; several ancient versions, and some early church fathers as well, have it.

The love of God for his elect is variously described in the New Testament. Here the purpose, or a purpose, of God in loving us is that we may be his children. And so we are, for God's purposes never fail and Christ shall see the results of the travail of his soul and shall be satisfied that he accomplished his purpose.

This entails what to some may appear as a disadvantage, namely, the world does not recognize us, does not know us, approve of us. Of course, in one sense the world knows us very well. At this writing the Internal Revenue Service has instituted rules to harass and very likely to suppress Christian elementary and high schools. Christian colleges have for some years suffered harassment. The courts incline to regard children as wards of the state and to deny parents their rightful authority in the upbringing of their offspring. Liberals who loudly assert that the Constitution erects a great wall of separation between church and state when Christians protest against abortion and homosexuality, never see a low fence when it comes to the State's curtailing the practice of religion. As one half drunk communist said to me as he was returning from Russia, "you can pray all you want." Yes, but you can't put your religion into practice.

What is the reason for this? John states it clearly: the IRS and the Supreme Court do not know God. They want to usurp his place as Father. From all appearances this liberalism—which is not liberalism at all, but reactionary totalitarianism—will increase. Hatred of Christ seemingly will wax worse and worse. We pray that totalitarianism, terrorism, socialism, and all the antichrists may be overthrown; but we have no indication that God will do so in the near future. Even the churches, the large liberal churches, contribute huge sums of money to support guerrilla warfare.

The final pronoun *him* refers to God, rather than to Christ. It is God in the first part of the verse, and God in the next verse. This is merely a matter of grammar, for Westcott's previous note indicates the inseparable unity between the Father and the Son.

> **3:2.   Beloved, we are now already children of God, but it is not yet evident what we shall be. We know that when it does become evident, we shall be like him, because we shall see him as he is.**

The translation: "when it does become evident" is better than "when he appears," because the verb in this phrase repeats the verb in the preceding phrase. Therefore, the subject should be the same.

If 2:20 be translated "you know all things," the *all* would have to be limited because here in 3:2 is something neither John, his addressees, nor we today know. We are indeed children of God, but our future state is unclear to us. In I Corinthians 15 the Apostle Paul gives an account of what the resurrection body will be. It will have no stomach, nor need for food. Christ himself said the marriage relation would not continue. Thus we know a little about that future life. John now tells us that we shall be like Christ because we shall see him as he is.

After the resurrection Christ's body was very different from what it had been. John 20:20 seems to say that when the disciples locked themselves in a room for fear of the Jews, Jesus appeared bodily in the room without opening the doors. Our present bodies cannot pass through wooden doors. Yet he showed them his hands and feet, and eight days later under the same circumstances invited Thomas to touch him. Luke 24:39ff. quotes him as saying, "Handle me and see, for a ghost hath not flesh and bones as ye see me have. Then he took some fish and ate it." The three mysterious strangers in Genesis 18, who seemingly appeared from nowhere, ate a meal of butter, milk, and beef. Did the Trinity eat? There were three men; but the three said, "I [singular] will return" and a few verses later "The Lord said." Then the men [plural] rose up and looked toward Sodom. But after the men had gone away, the Lord stood by Abraham. Very strange.

Though we do not now know the details of the similitude, yet we do know that we shall be like him, because we shall see God as he is. No man hath seen God at any time; and theological skeptics use the doctrine of transcendence to claim that God is in himself unknowable. Or they say we cannot know what God is, though we can know that he is; or we can know only his manifestations. Against this irrational mysticism the Scripture says that even now we live and move and have our being in God, in his light we see light, from which Calvin concludes that we must know God before we can know ourselves; and further, that we shall in the future see God as he is in his very essence. Of course, God is incorporeal, a pure spirit. There is nothing to see in the sense of optical chemistry on the retina. This seeing is purely intellectual. We see the Truth in all clarity.

No doubt many Christians believe that this passage refers to Christ's return. They translate *phanerōthē* as, when *he* shall appear. But please note, verse 1 speaks of the *Father,* and we are children of *God.* Again at the beginning of this verse also we are children of *God.* This is not a passage on Christ's return, but an anticipation of heaven—as the next verse also indicates.

3:3. And everyone who has this hope on him purifies himself as that one is pure.

The translation: "hope on him" not "has the hope in his heart," but has a hope whose object is God or heaven. That one *(ekeinos),* a pronoun pointing back to a previous, not the nearest, noun. Therefore, *ekeinos* means God.

All commentators, including the present writer, make mistakes. Here most of the commentators are against me. Bultmann writes, "*Ekeinos* of course refers to Jesus, who is designated as *ekeinos* here, in 2:6; 3:5, 7, 16; 4:17, and often in John." But this is like saying that the relative *who* or the pronoun *he* cannot refer to a given person because in other sentences it refers to another person. In 2:6 *ekeinos* must mean Jesus, not because it is the word *ekeinos,* but because it refers to someone who *walked.* In 3:5 *ekeinos* took away sin. This idea controls 3:7 also. Verse 16 refers to the crucifixion and so must mean Christ. Verse 4:17 is doubtful. In every case who *ekeinos* is, is to be determined by the context, not by the pronoun itself.

However, since the majority are against me, I shall quote the somewhat extended argument of A. W. Pink. Then the reader must judge for himself.

> There is as usual some difficulty here as to the pronouns *Him* and *He.* The first *Him* evidently points to God the Father, whose children we are. The hope which we have of being like God, because we shall see him as he is, is a hope in *Him* or upon *Him,* having *Him* as its object and its ground. It is the last *He* that may seem uncertain. It is a different word in the original from the previous word *Him;* which again is the same as that used in the previous verse about God. The *He* in the close of the verse—*even as he is pure*—is emphatically demonstrative. It means *that one, that child of God, that Son.* So clear is the identification of the person. Both pronouns, it is to be noticed—the *Him* and the

He—are expressed in the original, and not left to be supplied. The first naturally refers to the person previously spoken of, God the Father, whose children we are. The second as naturally refers to some other person, already distinctly enough indicated, in whom the ideal of our ultimate perfection in respect of likeness to God is realized, and in whom therefore the model and standard of our duty as aiming at that likeness is to be found. That person is evidently Christ the Son. The verse, accordingly, interpreted in strict consistency with the exact grammatical construction, may and must run thus: Every man, every one, every child of God—having this hope in God, the hope of seeing him as he is and being like him—purifies himself, even as that child of God, that Son of God, that Christ, is pure. (p. 108)

With all this tedious argument about a pronoun one can easily overlook a point that is rather obscurely referred to in the verse. Parts of Scriptures frequently enough contain implications that escape notice by reason of their being on situations not alluded to in the text. Verse 3 says that a man who entertains the hope of heaven (or the hope of seeing Christ, if you wish, for this point does not depend on the identification of *ekeinos*) purifies or is purifying himself. Now, it is easy to surmise that a Christian in whom this hope is vigorous will be strengthened against temptation and encouraged in righteousness. But could a Wesleyan, who considers himself to have arrived at a state of sinless perfection, have this hope of heaven? He is no longer purifying himself. Hope of heaven inevitably causes a process of purification; but if anyone were sinless, such a process would have ceased. Strange, is it not?

3:4.   Everyone who does sin also does lawlessness, for sin is lawlessness.

The translation: The term *for* is rather an interpretation than a literal translation. Literally, it is "and."

At this point some editors begin a new paragraph; some do not. Similarly, some make a break between verses 6 and 7, and others do not. Again, outlining this Epistle is difficult.

The real difficulty with the Wesleyans, just previously mentioned, is that they don't know what sin is. The gentleman of such fine Christian character who claimed not to have sinned in the previous 26 years acknowledged that of course he made mistakes. Romanism distinguishes between venial and mortal sins. Others talk about conscious sins and unfortunate actions done unwittingly. Now while the Scriptures assert degrees of heinousness, they also impose judgment on all. A baby is born sinful. He has inherited a lawless nature from Adam. We were shapened in iniquity and in sin did our mothers conceive us. Who can understand his errors? Cleanse thou me from secret faults.

Some remarks were made earlier about legalism. God is supposed to be affronted by forensic concepts. Nonsense! Law determines what sin is. By the law is the knowledge of sin. Sin is not imputed where there is no law. The law is our schoolmaster to bring us to Christ; and after we come to Christ, a young man cleanses his way by taking heed to God's Word and statutes. Sin is any deviation from the law—any want of conformity unto or transgression of the law of God. While we should indeed condemn known sins, we should not refrain from condemning unknown sins. Sin is lawlessness, whether we know the law or not. A person who says he has not sinned for 26 years, or 26 minutes, just does not know what sin is. It behooves us to pay attention to the scriptural definition. When one is fuzzy on the definitions, one is fuzzy.

3:5.   And you know that that one (*ekeinos*) was revealed in order to take away sins, and there is no sin in him (*autō*).

Here *oidamen* can be termed "absolute," for it is certainly not based on observation. No one learns by experience that Jesus was crucified to expiate sin. This knowledge comes only by verbal revelation.

Ekeinos certainly refers to Christ; not because this demonstrative must refer to Christ, but because the one spoken of is the one who took away sins. The next pronoun is *autō*, and this refers to Christ as well. It is the context that determines to whom the pronoun refers.

Perhaps it is worthy of note that the phrase "there is no sin in him" has a verb in the present tense. Had the verse referred simply to his earthly ministry, it would have said, there was no sin in him. The present indicates a continuing, or eternal, condition. We might have guessed as much, even if the verb had been aorist or imperfect; but the present is a slight indication of something more than past.

3:6. Everyone who remains in him does not sin. Everyone who sins has not seen him nor known him.

This verse and another a bit further down have been used by Wesleyans to support sinless perfection. If the present indicative and present participle are taken in such a sense, it would follow that only sinless and perfect people have known Christ. On this showing 99 percent of the most devout and orthodox believers have neither seen him nor known him.

That John had no such thought in mind is perfectly clear from 1:8, 9. In fact, John in those verses says not only that his addressees sin, he acknowledges that he himself sins. The explanation should be well known: the present tense can and here must refer to habitual conduct. It does not have to do with sporadic acts of sinning. There is an English parallel. One may say that so and so is living in sin. This does not mean occasional acts, even occasional acts of fornication; but an established mode of life. F. F. Bruce offers a good illustration: "When a boy goes to a new school, he may inadvertently do something out of keeping with the school's tradition or good name, to be told immediately, 'That isn't done here.' A literalist might reply, 'But obviously it *is* done; this boy has just done it'; but he would be deliberately missing the point of the rebuke" (p. 90).

When the verse says that the habitual sinner has not seen Christ, it is not making the assertion that the sinner did not see Jesus walking around Galilee. This "seeing" is not sensory but intellectual. The verse applies to people in all ages. Indeed, probably none of John's addressees had visually seen Jesus. *See* and *know* are here synonymous. Once more *ginōskō* cannot mean knowledge by observation, for all of John's children, that is, most of his congregation, had "seen" and known the Lord.

3:7. Children, let no one deceive you. He who does justice is just, as that one is just.

Here *ekeinos* refers to Christ because it refers to *ekeinos* in verse 5, and in verse 5 *ekeinos* indicates the one who takes away sin. It is not the pronoun itself that gives it its meaning, but the context.

It seems that the heretics whom John is combating not only denied the incarnation but also lived unrighteous lives. Whether there was some one sin which they conspicuously committed, or whether they were in general unrighteous, cannot be determined by the text. But it does seem that they were leading some of the congregation into evil ways. Perhaps we can surmise that the sins in view were not conspicuously immoral, for in such a case deception would have been unlikely, or less likely. If one may choose an example from present day affairs, it could be subtle compromise with modernism. There are two cases. Members of unbelieving denominations remain enmeshed because their local congregation seems sound. They even excuse themselves by saying that none of the congregational money goes to the denomination. This statement is almost always false. But even if it were true, it misses the main point: namely, they give their personal adherence to an apostate church, and they fail to see that this personal support, regardless of money, is sin. It also leads others to sin because their conduct obscures the great chasm between faith and unbelief. The second case is similar. A session in an orthodox denomination may decide to cooperate with a session in an apostate denomination, on the assumption that the latter session is itself sound. Of course, the latter session is not sound, or it would not remain unequally yoked to unbelievers. Then in the cooperative evangelistic campaign, or whatever activity it may be, some persons who had never before confessed Christ may do so and unite with the apostate denomination. At best this results in stunted growth or a later falling away. Let no one deceive you: if a session does not act righteously and does not renounce unbelief, something is sadly amiss.

3:8. He who lives in sin belongs to the devil and the devil sins from the beginning. To this end the Son of God was revealed, viz., to destroy the works of the devil.

Calvin remarks,

> The Pelagians, indeed, and the Catharians did formerly make a wrong use of this passage, when they vainly imagined that the faithful are in this world endued with angelic purity; and in our own age some of the Anabaptists have renewed this dotage. But all those who dream of a perfection of this kind, sufficiently show what stupid consciences they

> must have. But the words of the Apostle are so far from countenancing their error that they are sufficient to refute it.

Perhaps here we can indulge ourselves with another example of Bultmann's subjective analyses. I shall omit the Greek, but in every other respect the quotation is verbatim:

> If v. 8 derives from the Source, then there is some question with respect to v. 7b. The phrase of v. 7b "he who does right" appears to take up the sentence from 2:29 once again, since it forms antithetical parallelism with "he who commits sin" in v. 9; one is inclined therefore to assign it to the Source. The continuation "he is righteous," however, is remarkably weak. In accordance with 2:29 one expects "is born of God," and if v. 7 really came from the Source, that might have been the original conclusion of the sentence, which the author altered to "he is righteous." In any case "just as that one is righteous" stems from the author.

How gracious of Bultmann to allow the unknown author to have written some of the Epistle without having copied and altered an equally unknown source! Bultmann explains in his Introduction:

> The decisive argument against this identification [of the author of the Gospel with the author of the Epistle] is the following: the Gospel of John and I John are directed against different fronts. Whereas the Gospel is opposed to the "world," or to the Jews who are its representatives, and therefore to non-Christians, the false teachers who are opposed to I John are within the Christian community. . . . This shows that I John originates in a period later than the Gospel.

Of course, it is possible that I John is later than the Gospel, for even the liberal scholar Albright found no internal evidence for dating the Gospel later than A.D. 70. But Butlmann places the Gospel very late and therefore the Epistle would come in the second century. However, Bultmann's main point is that these two New Testament books could not have been written by the same author because they are addressed to two different groups of people. Dear Reader: Did you ever address two letters to two different persons on two different subjects? This passage from Bultmann, his reconstructions of the text, his repeated discoveries of several authors, sources, editors, and errors, his entire subjective methodology, deserves only to be satirized. A mimeographed sheet has made the round, doing so. It seems to have been written by Jack Lindquist, who deserves credit both for his wit and his understanding of these literary methods. I do not know whether it has appeared in print anywhere, and I hope I am not violating any copyright laws, but it deserves reproduction, and I acknowledge the author enthusiastically.

BULTMANN READS MOTHER GOOSE

I—A   Hey diddle-diddle,
I—B   The cat and the fiddle,
II—A   The cow jumped over the moon.
II—B   The little dog laughed to see such sport,
III   And the dish ran away with the spoon.

1. *Authorship and Date.* Internal evidence rejects the view that we have here an original composition by Mary (Mother) Goose of Boston (1686-1743).[1] The phrasing of I-A is definitely *late* eighteenth century, since the Goose Period would have rendered it "didd*ley*-didd*ley*" (and thus "fiddley" in I-B). Furthermore, the sequence "cat-cow-dog-dish" represents an obvious redaction and is a compilation of at least four different accounts.[2] Thus, the author of the piece is unknown,[3] and its date set between 1780 and 1820.[4] The *Sitz im Leben* of the Depression of 1815 may be reflected in III.

2. *Text.* The received text is very corrupt. The mythological element in II-A is typical of many other interpolations, as is the anthropomorphism in II-B.[5] However, I-A may be original, excluding, of course, the "hey."[6]

3. *Interpretation.* Stripped of its thought forms, the piece tells us of something revolutionary as existentially encountered by three animals, two cooking implements, and one musical instrument.[7]

---

[1]Discussed in F. Saurkraut, *Gooses Werke*, Vol. XXVII, pp. 825-906; G.F.W. Steinbauger, *Gooserbrief*, pp. 704-863; *Festschrift fur Baron von Munchausen*, pp. XIII-XX; R. Pretzlebender, *Die Goosensinger vom Boston*, p. 106.

[2]See P. Katzenjammer in *Goosengeschichtliche Schule Jahrbuch*, Vol. X.

[3]Some attribute it to Mary's grandson, Wild Goose (1793-1849), and others to Wild Goose's nephew, Cooked (1803-1865). Both views are challenged by A. Kegdrainer in the thirty volume prolegomenon, *Gooseleiden*, Vol. XV.

[4]F. Pfeffernusse contends it is an English translation of a German original by the infant Wagner. See his *Goose und Volkgeist*, pp. 38-52; also his *Geist und Volkgoose*, pp. 27-46.

[5]The authenticity of both II-A and II-B is poorly argued by the reactionary American Goosologist, Carl Sandbag in his *Old Glory and Mother Goose* (see Vol. IV. *The Winters in the South*, p. 357).

[6]The meaning of the word "hey" is now hopelessly obscure. See my articles on "Hey, that ain't" and "Hey, What the" in *Goosengrease*, Fall, 1942.

[7]Perhaps an eclipse of the moon?

Less witty than Mr. Lindquist, the present writer calls attention to the logic of Bultmann's denial of Johannine authorship. For him the fact that the Gospel was addressed to the world, while the Epistle was addressed to the church, is "the decisive argument against this identification" of the author of the Gospel with the author of the Epistle. If this is good logic, the present writer could not have written *The Philosophy of Science and Belief in God*, directed against atheistic scientists, because he surely wrote *I Corinthians, A Contemporary Commentary* for the edification of Christians.

Probably no commentator deduces a philosophic dualism from this verse. The argument would have to be: if the devil sins from the beginning, and the Logos was in the beginning with God, then both Christ and the devil are eternal. It would be difficult to find a theologian so stupid as to imagine the two beginnings were identical. Of course, Christianity is monistic, not dualistic. There is only one original source. The devil was a creation. But he sinned, perhaps not from the date of his creation, but he sinned from the beginning of sin. He was the first sinner. This probably is the correct interpretation of the conjunction *because*. Because the devil was the first, sinners today can be called his posterity.

The last phrase of the verse hardly needs explanation. It states one purpose, the most obvious purpose, of the incarnation. The reason Christ assumed human nature was to destroy the works of the devil. When born, his name was to be Jesus, for he shall save his people from their sins. The verb in this verse is properly translated *destroy*. More literally it means *to loose*, as the disciples loosed the colt in Matthew 21:2. If now we dare to be pleasantly pictorial, we may imagine that the devil has tied us into knots, and Christ has come to untie them. Still pictorial, we can say that we are bound by sin and that Christ strikes off our fetters. Of course, Christ had a complex of purposes, but this one affects us most directly.

3:9.   Everyone who has been begotten of God does not sin, because his seed remains in him, and he cannot sin, because he has been begotten of God.

Translation and punctuation: The first phrase, in literal translation, should in good English read: No one begotten of God commits sin. Instead of three commas, the KJV has a semicolon, a colon, and a comma. The RSV has a semicolon, a comma, and nothing. The NASB has a comma, a semicolon, and a comma. It seems best, simply because of English style, to omit the first and third punctuation marks. The middle mark could then be either a comma or a semicolon.

Remember: there are no punctuation marks in the manuscripts. The result is that there are two statements, each followed by an explanation.

If the first of these statements were understood in its literal English, the ordinary Wesleyan doctrine of a higher stage of Christian life in which no sin occurs, would, as earlier explained, be refuted. The reason is that this verse does not limit itself to elderly saints, but applies to everyone who has been born again. The most recently converted sinner would be instantaneously sinless. Since the apostle very clearly said that all Christians sin, this verse means, and Greek usage permits it, that the true Christian is not an habitual sinner.

There is a similar distinction in Romans 6, so that the form of expression here is not suspiciously unique. W. G. T. Shedd in his commentary makes these pertinent observations:

> Ver. 16: Compare 2 Peter ii.19. The argument here is derived from the nature of the human will, and of voluntary agency. Purpose and inclination in one direction are incompatible with purpose and inclination in the contrary direction. It is the argument of Christ in Matt. vi.24; vii.18: No man can serve two masters. The connection of thought is as follows: "Because you have died with Christ for sin and are delivered from condemnation and have a full title to eternal reward, you are obligated by such gracious treatment not to yield yourselves to the lusts that remain, but to yield yourselves to the holy law of God. . . ." (p. 162)

Then on page 166 he continues:

> Slaves of righteousness. . . . This also is an inability to the contrary resulting from a foregoing act and state of the will. Holy inclination is inability to sin. . . . A will which by regeneration has been "powerfully determined" (Westminster L. C. 67) and inclined to holiness is unable to sin, in the sense in which Christ intends when he says that "a good tree cannot bring forth evil fruit" (Matt. vii.18); and in which St. John intends when he asserts that the regenerate "cannot sin, because he is born of God."

So much for Shedd on Romans and our present verse.

Now the difference between our present verse (3:9) and verse 6 just above is that here a reason is given. The Christian is not an inveterate sinner because God's seed remains in him. Some commentators have tried to hold that it is the Christian's seed that remains in him. This hardly makes any sense. It is the seed of God.

But it is important to know precisely what this seed is. Cotton, Westcott, and Lenski agree that this seed is the word—the Scripture. Neither Bruce nor Stott is very clear in his exposition, except that each clearly does not identify the seed with the Scriptures. The others support that view by an appeal to James 1:18, "Of his own will begat he us with the word of truth."

I Peter 1:23 reads, "Born again, not of corruptible seed, but of incorruptible, by the word of God which liveth and abideth forever." Then in the Gospels, by which these later verses may have been inspired, Luke 3:11, 12, 15 says, "The seed is the word of God . . . and they having heard the word keep it." Keeping the word, as in Luke, is the same thought as John's: the seed or word remains in him.

The verse concludes by emphasizing the thoughts in reverse order: he cannot go on sinning because he has been begotten of God.

3:10.   By this the children of God and the children of the devil are clearly distinguished—everyone who does not act righteously is not of God, and he who does not love his brother.

Some outlines begin a new paragraph with this verse. Others start with its last phrase. Still others make verse 11 the first of a new section. Another starts the new section at 13. At any rate, somewhere along in here John shifts to the theme of love of the brethren.

One of the distinguishing features of a Christian is his love of the brethren. It is not the only one, for obviously the Christian's love of God is another. Furthermore, the verse seems to present us with two criteria: righteousness and love. Nor, clearly, is it to be supposed that love of the brethren so exhausts acting righteously that other sins are permissible. Righteousness and love are intimately connected, and somewhere or other we must see how. But here love of the brethren receives the emphasis.

A New Testament example of this love would be the relief that poor Christians elsewhere sent to the still poorer famine sufferers in Jerusalem. It is hard to imagine the Vestal Virgins in Rome sending contributions to suffering Elusinians in Greece. At any rate Caligula and Nero never would have done so.

As a general rule people, including Christians, are not too generous. Hence, this love needs emphasis today. At the same time there are a few examples of the opposite extreme. On one occasion my car needed some minor tinkering. A very poor student understood cars much better than what was required for this job. But he absolutely refused payment because he and I were both Christians: he was showing his Christian love to a brother. I did not appreciate this. I was well able to pay, and a workman is worthy of his hire. My love for him consisted in asking him to do the work instead of taking the car to a garage. In fact, I would benefit from his lower charge. I intended to give him more work later on. But his misguided notion of love prevented further arrangements. We both suffered.

A second example is quite the reverse of this. A very poorly paid minister whose wife had to use food stamps had in his congregation a still poorer family. They lived in a trailer. The woman never cooked a meal and hardly ever cleaned the place. She came to church regularly, but borrowed money she never repaid. After the pastor had given her more money than he should have, and refused her next request, she complained that he should show more Christian love. A few weeks later, penniless, she tried to buy a large house and turn it into a sort of orphanage—this woman who never cooked and hardly ever cleaned. We are indeed to love the brethren, but sometimes love demands us to teach others their responsibilities.

In fact, love, as commonly understood is useless. A bride may love her young husband, but her love does not tell her how to bake a cherry pie. Her husband needs information as how to replace a washer on the sink; love alone gives no direction. But Christian love gives directions because Christian love is obedience to the laws and precepts in the Bible. Only recently has love been regarded as an emotion. For 15 centuries or so Christian theologians have understood love to be a volition. With the advent of Freud, volition disappeared and frightful emotions took over. The Christian populace have been unwittingly affected by this behaviorism, and they should immediately return to the biblical position.

3:11. Because this is the message which you heard from the beginning: that we love one another.

Surely those outlines that start a new paragraph with this verse are clumsy. It is not a complete sentence: it must be tacked on to the end of verse 10. The idea is that love distinguishes Christians from others because the precept of love is a part of the original Christian message.

3:12.   Not as Cain was of the evil one and murdered his brother. And why did he murder him? Because his works were evil, but his brother's were righteous.

In order to form a sharp contrast with love, John adduces the hatred of Cain. The contrast cannot be misunderstood. But in this present age something needs to be said about the "evil one" under whose instigation Cain acted. Not many people today believe in a devil. Perhaps a few weirdos have resurrected devil-worship, but the Western world by a great majority dismisses all such notions as mythology. The Scripture, however, and John in particular have no doubts about his reality. Already the Epistle has mentioned the devil three times, the evil one twice (2:13, 14), and after the present verse twice more (5:18, 19). In addition, the term *diabolos* occurs in 3:8, 10. John's Gospel mentions the devil twice (8:44, 13:2) and the evil one (presumably) in 17:15. Those who wish may check the references in other New Testament books, also. In fact, II Kings 6:17, Ephesians 1:21, 2:2, 10, and Jude 9 warn us not to believe that sensory objects are the only or most important elements in the world.

As for the main thought in the verse, it is so clear that comment is hardly needed. Wicked men hate righteous men. Abortionists hate Christians; homosexuals hate Anita Bryant; and communists want to crush all religion. Always remember that a Christian is a person whom the world hates; and Christ said, "ye know that it hated me before it hated you." This statement was probably in John's mind as he wrote the next verse.

3:13.   Do not be surprised, brethren, if the world hates you.

Abel was, no doubt, surprised. He and Cain were brothers. They had played and grown up together. Their parents had told both of them about the garden of Eden, their fall, and the necessity of a sacrifice for sin. The two boys, as they grew up, took up their occupations, one tending the fields, the other the cattle. How could one hate the other? Would not Abel have been much surprised and disturbed to discover, little by little, that his brother hated him, really hated him? But by Christ's day, and even more so now, no one should be surprised that evil men hate good men. As Isaac Watts said in a hymn we do not sing,

> Dogs delight to bark and bite,
> For 'tis their nature to.

This, however, is a travesty on dogs. It is human beings that bark and bite, for 'tis their nature to. Do not be surprised.

3:14. We know that we have passed from death to life because we love the brethren. He who does not love (his brother) remains in death.

Textual note. Many manuscripts have "his brother"; the opposing evidence is not sufficient to exclude the two words.

This seemingly simple verse is really very difficult to understand, and most commentators dodge the difficulties. Like all others, this verse must be explained in its context. But unlike some verses, hardly anything can be said of it by itself. Therefore, let us immediately connect it with the verse that follows.

3:15. Everyone who hates his brother is a murderer, and you know that every murderer has no eternal life remaining in him.

Some very cautious Christians dislike having their attention called to difficulties. Probably even more they wish for silence so as not to cause doubt or weaken the faith of weaker brothers. But is it love to deceive even immature Christians? Is it edifying to hide problems from the more mature? This is in itself one of the difficulties in these verses. What is love? What does it require? Surely, not deceit and evasion. Then must we say that these cautious Christians are not true Christians because their evasions show they have no love? Or maybe, only a little love? How much love, then, is necessary before we can know that we have passed from death to life?

A commentator who raises such difficulties is often misunderstood, and the timid brother begins to think him a disciple of Cerinthus. Now, let it be known that the present writer does not encourage or condone murder. The text says, or seems to say, that no murderer has eternal life.

There are two difficulties here, a less important and a more important one. First, if a murderer has no eternal life remaining in him, are we to suppose he earlier had eternal life and then lost it? The doctrine of the perseverance of the saints is involved here. Lenski, who presumably does not believe in perseverance, remarks that this point is immaterial (p. 470). We may allow that it is not emphasized in this verse; yet it is hardly immaterial, for a life that can be lost is not eternal. Further, this point is not absent from the more important difficulty.

So, second, aside from the question whether or not a child of God loses his sonship when he commits murder, there is the question whether a child of God can possibly commit murder in the first place. Here then is the problem: Did David lose salvation when he murdered Uriah, or was he never a child of God until afterward?

Now, F. F. Bruce has a widespread reputation as a scholar, and Stott is a prolific writer, but neither of them faces up to the difficulty. Westcott passes by in trivialities. Yet the two verses begin with an emphatic, "We know." Bultmann calls it a "strong—one may say arrogant—expression." Does John contradict the Old Testament? Most people think that David was regenerate before he committed his great sin. Are they all mistaken?

John Cotton notices the difficulty. He seems to start upon a solution, but he can hardly be said to have completed it, or at least he left it vague. "What of David and others in their carnal state? David did indeed kill . . . but upon repentance God forgave him his sin. . . . As John speaks not of every murderer, for some do it against their judgments and hearts; but others, if they repent not, have not eternal life."

Cotton is undoubtedly correct, but to alleviate the apparent contradiction with the Old Testament, the only recourse seems to be to take the present tense of "he who hates" and the noun "murderer" as designating habitual thoughts and actions. English does not use this sense as often as Greek, but even in English, when we say "he is a thief," we do not mean that he committed a theft yesterday, but that he habitually steals. Or when we say a man hates, we mean more than a single, unusual act of hatred.

There are other and worse difficulties in these verses. John "arrogantly" said *we* (in contradistinction to others) *know* because we love. That very evangelistic minister who cheated on his wife, deserted her, and married another girl, at one time "knew" he was saved. He put great stress on experience. He entertained no doubts, neither about himself nor about his congregation because the Holy Spirit had given him the gift of discerning the hearts of men. Well, maybe he will someday repent, as David did; but at present God alone knows. Surely the minister himself does not know. Now you and I have never committed adultery (in the legal sense, apart from Christ's wider interpretation), but do we know we never shall; and do we know that if we do, we will later repent?

Of course, we can be *assured* of our salvation. An Arminian friend of mine claimed to have assurance—assurance that if he died on the spot, he would go to heaven. But if he should live until tomorrow he might fall from grace during the night. He clearly did not *know* he would be granted eternal bliss. Probably there are also persons who profess to believe in "eternal security," and who claim to have both love and faith. They are assured. But, first, other people are sure that drinking vinegar cures warts and that laetril cures cancer. Being assured does not make it so. Then there is Louis Berkhof who lists a dozen different kinds of faith. One of them is "temporary" faith; though he carefully explains that temporary faith can be permanent.

Charles Hodge has some good things to say about assurance, but he dodges the main issue. On pages 106-7 of Volume III he writes: "To make assurance of personal salvation essential to faith is contrary to Scripture and to the experience of God's people. The Bible speaks of a weak faith. . . . Those who make assurance the essence of faith generally reduce faith to a mere intellectual assent."

Aside from the pejorative term *mere*, this is essentially Calvin's position. For him a person without assurance has no faith at all. Anyone who believed knew he believed and was *ipso facto* assured. But to continue Hodge: ". . . Scripture and experience teach that assurance is not only attainable, but a privilege and a duty. There may indeed be assurance, where there is no true faith at all."

Here is the difficulty Hodge does not face. How can one know that his assurance is not a delusion?

> But where there is true faith, the want of assurance is to be referred either to the weakness of faith or to erroneous views of the plan of salvation. Many sincere believers are too introspective. They look too exclusively within, so that their hope is graduated by the degree of evidence of regeneration which they find in their own experience. . . . We may examine our hearts with all the microscopic care prescribed by President Edwards . . . and never be satisfied that we have eliminated every ground of misgiving and doubt.

Hodge continues by listing five grounds of assurance—external, not internal grounds. But the reader must judge for himself whether or not Hodge has eliminated every ground of misgiving and doubt. In fact, while Hodge's external grounds are exceedingly important, and usually underemphasized, ignored, or even explicitly denied in contemporary pietism, our text in John's Epistle certainly seems to depend on internal factors and our mental ability to arrive at a correct psychological analysis of them. Does regeneration guarantee competence in psychology? It must be admitted, therefore, that these apparently simple verses are in truth immensely difficult.

3:16.   In this we know love, that that one laid down his soul for us; and we should lay down our souls for the brethren.

The questions, What is love? and What does it require? have previously arisen. Here is not a definition but an example of love: Christ died for us. This is not Mary Baker Eddy's notion of love. Her teaching on the atonement is no more Christian than a human sacrifice to Shiva; possibly less so. But should we likewise sacrifice ourselves for our brethren? In one sense, we cannot. Our death would never expiate their sins. While we to a certain extent must imitate Christ, there are some things about him we cannot imitate. We can, in certain situations, lay down our life for the brethren. If our death should allow 10 Christians to escape death, should we not do so? Some Hollanders risked and lost their lives for Jews who were not brethren. But let us pray that none of us be put to such a test.

In opposition to that contemporary Christianity which has been infected by Freudian psychology, this love is not an emotion. It is an intellectual conviction that results in an act of volition. In times of persecution, as in Uganda recently, frothy emotion has no place. Nor in other times, either.

More familiar to us Americans than the severities inflicted on Christians under communistic and dictatorial governments, are situations in which love is expressed in sacrifices less than death. This comes up in the next verse.

3:17.   He who has the life of the world and sees his brother in need and locks up his compassion from him, how does the love of God remain in Him?

The translation: It may be a matter of curiosity that the term *life* in the phrase "the life of the world," does not mean the physiological functions, but rather the manner of living. It also means wine made from ripe grapes. But here it refers to "the world we live in," as opposed to the ethereal regions in which philosophers ascend to Aristophanes' clouds; more exactly the verse refers to the means of livelihood. The usual translation is quite correct: "the world's goods." What may be more useful for New Testament exegesis is the usage of the word *cosmos*. The term *world* has several different meanings in the New Testament.

As for the sense of the verse, we have here a sacrifice much less than death. When we, who have food enough and to spare, see another Christian on the verge of starvation, we should exercise compassion and feed him and his family. In winter we should give him our half-worn overcoat and buy a new one for ourselves. Or should we really buy him a new one and make our old one go through another season? In this very vicinity there is a "ghetto" congregation that does a great deal of such work. Of course, it is not a ghetto; it is a very poor congregation; *ghetto* is simply a propaganda word that has been wrenched from its original meaning for political purposes.

A person who lacks compassion lacks the love of God. This is surely an objective genitive: he does not love God. Stott's attempt to defend a subjective genitive—God does not love him—is unconvincing. If God loved David through his sin and granted him the gift of repentance, God no doubt loves unloving Christians and grants them repentance also. Lenski's interpretation is correct.

3:18. Children, let us not love in word or tongue, but in deed and truth.

This verse serves a dual purpose. As an exhortation it rounds off the preceding; but it also introduces a new paragraph. Plummer's outline had: (c) Love and Hate, 3:18-24. The other outline had: 2. Christ's Sacrifice, an Example, 3:16-18; (3) Love Gives Confidence, 3:18-23. Note, the two outlines neither begin nor end together. The verse deplores hypocrisy, and further explanation is unnecessary.

3:19, 20. By this we shall know that we are of the truth, and before him we shall persuade our heart that if our heart condemn us that God is greater than our heart and he knows everything.

The translation: Since verse 20 consists of two dependent clauses, the two verses must be a single sentence. But the verb *persuade* may be translated *assure*, and this changes the status of the first dependent clause. The second is difficult in either case. These difficulties in translation are equally difficulties in interpretation.

First, let us examine some standard translations. Note the wording and even the punctuation.

KJV: And hereby we know that we are of the truth, and shall assure our hearts before him. For if our heart condemn us, God is greater than our heart, and knoweth all things.

RSV: By this we shall know that we are of the truth, and reassure our hearts before him whenever our hearts condemn us; for God is greater than our hearts, and he knows everything.

NASB: We shall know by this that we are of the truth, and shall assure our heart before him, in whatever our heart condemns us; for God is greater than our heart, and knows all things.

Now, though it is not a "standard translation," let us see what Westcott did with the verse:

In this we shall know that we are of the truth, and shall assure our heart before him, whereinsoever our heart may condemn us; because God is greater than our heart and knoweth all things.

These translations seem to say that if we give our overcoat to a shivering fellow Christian in the ghetto, we can be assured in *whatever* our heart condemns us—for example, our burglary to get the coat in the first place—that God will not condemn us.

Against this lax view John Cotton takes a very strict position: "According to the verdict or testimony of our consciences, God will save us or condemn us at the last day. If our hearts condemn us, God knows more against us to condemn us" (p. 385). Yet on the next page he also says, "If you see one spark of sincerity in yourself, God sees more." This sentence in itself is very comforting. If we really feel sorry for the man in poverty, God sees more sparks of sincerity and we shall be saved by giving the stolen coat. But Cotton oscillates: "Conscience sometimes bears false witness (Titus 1:15, 16). If a man has a defiled conscience, it will deal falsely." This is not so comforting; especially if a defiled conscience is ignorant of its defilement, which is ordinarily the case. Yet, though Cotton recognizes that consciences are defiled, he can say, "if conscience acquits you, then will God much more." But again, on the next page he adds, "Our hearts make us believe we are rich and have need of nothing, when indeed we are wretched and miserable, poor, blind, and naked . . . while we walk in a sinful way they make us believe we are in God's favor." It looks as if we can find no help in such a confused commentator.

Westcott, whose translation appears a few paragraphs above, canvasses the difficulties. They need to be considered with care.

The many conflicting interpretations of this passage spring out of different translations of (1) the verb *peisomen*, and (2) the double conjunction or relative *oti* (*o ti*).

I. Thus if we take the sense *persuade* for the verb, there are two groups of rendering possible: the first (a) in which the clauses which follow give the substance of that of which we are satisfied, and the second (b) in which this substance is supposed to be supplied by the reader.

(a) In the first case there are two possible views:

(i) The second *oti* may be simply resumptive: We shall persuade our heart that, if our heart condemn us, that, I say, God is greater. . . .

(ii) Or the first *oti* may be taken as the relative: We shall persuade our heart, whereinsoever our heart condemns us, that God is greater. . . .

Against both these interpretations it may be urged, as it seems, with decisive force, that the conclusion is not one which flows naturally from the premise. The consciousness of a sincere love of the brethren does not furnish the basis of the conviction of the sovereign greatness of God.

(b) If the substance of that of which we shall be persuaded is mentally supplied, as, 'that we are of the truth,' or 'that our prayers are heard,' there are again two possible interpretations.

(i) The second *oti* may be taken as resumptive in the sense *because:* we shall persuade our heart because if our heart condemn us, because, I say, God is greater. . . .

It appears to be a fatal objection to both these views that just that has to be supplied which the sense given to the verb leads the reader to expect to be clearly expressed. And further, it may be remarked that while the use of a resumptive *oti* is quite intelligible after the introduction of a considerable clause, it is very unnatural after the insertion of a few words.

2. If on the other hand the verb be taken in the sense 'we shall still and tranquillise the fears and misgivings of our heart, there are yet two modes of completing the sentence:

(a) The second *oti* may be taken as resumptive in the sense of *because:* we shall assure our hearts because if our heart condemn us, because, I say, God is greater. Such a resumptive use of the particle has however been shown to be very harsh.

(b) There remains then the adoption of the first relative: We shall assure our heart, whereinsoever our heart condemn us because God is greater.

This sense falls in completely with the context and flows naturally from the Greek.

There is another paragraph from Westcott still to be quoted; but permit this interruption. Arndt and Gingrich allow that *ean* "sometimes approaches the meaning of *when.*" This is true even in English. "If you come" and "when you come" are almost the same, except that "when" assumes you are coming, while "if" leaves it in doubt. This degree of doubt is not important in the present tense. But the translation *whereinsoever* is so broad that it inclines us to pass over lightly the theft or murder we committed yesterday. Westcott recognizes this difficulty in his final paragraph.

> But an ambiguity still remains. In what sense is the superior greatness of God to be understood? Is it the ground of our exceeding need? or of our sure confidence? Both interpretations can be drawn from the words. (1) We shall then, and then only, still our heart, in whatsoever it may condemn us because we know that the judgment of God must be severer than our own judgment, and so apart from fellowship with him we can have no hope. Or (2) We shall then still our heart in whatsoever it may condemn us because we are in fellowship with God, and that fact assures us of his sovereign mercy. The latter sense seems to be required by the whole context.

What the internal conscience of murderers is like, the present writer does not profess to know. Murder does not seem to trouble the Mafia. But then it is doubtful that they claim fellowship with God or love of the brethren. However, Charles II and even the Huguenot Henri IV thought that God did not begrudge them a little adultery now and then. But suppose that Henri IV had a twinge of conscience under the preaching of his pastor—and his pastor did indeed rebuke him. Would he have replied, True, my heart condemns me, but God is greater than my heart? But suppose Henri never had a twinge of conscience—which seems rather to have been the case—could he have quoted the next verse: if my heart does not condemn me, God gives me his approval? Does not this absurdity tell heavily against Westcott's interpretation?

Now, it must be acknowledged that the context aims to give John's addressees confidence before God, rather than to frighten them by stressing God's severity. The first phrase is, "By this we shall know that we are of the truth." A knowledge that God is more severe in his judgments of us than we are, is hardly a ground of assurance or source of comfort. Yet what can "he knows all things" mean? Does it mean that God knows extenuating circumstances? This is something we know only too well, and the Scripture has little sympathy with extenuating circumstances. The nearest it comes is to assess responsibility and punishment in proportion to knowledge. And even here the ignorant servant is not excused; he is merely beaten with fewer stripes.

It is doubtful that these difficulties can or should be lessened by noticing that the first verb is in the future tense. The verse says, We shall know; it does not say, We know. *Peisomen* is also future, whether we translate it *persuade* or *assure*. But the difficulties remain, whether present or future.

Some help may come by attaching the first two words to the preceding verse. The *this* of "By this" is not to be found in verse 19, but in verse 18. If we love in deed and not in hypocritical professions, we shall know. This eliminates the Mafia and most murderers. But does it eliminate Henri IV? He could claim that he loved the Huguenots, and only by submitting to the Pope could he save them from war and persecution. So his affairs with several mistresses are of no importance.

This introduces a serious difficulty most commentators ignore. How can we know we love the brethren? The Scriptures tell us we should love even our enemies. But then what about the civil liberty's lawyer who insisted that Christians should love the Soviet Mongol soldiers who massacred the patriotic Hungarians back in the fifties? Should we not rather have loved the oppressed Hungarians? Similarly, the modernists, as they attacked the Scripture and turned their denominations into synagogues of Satan, charged the fundamentalists with a lack of love: the latter were so censorious of those blameless and blessed pastors who denied the virgin birth and the atonement. The liberals could have, and are beginning to accuse Martin Luther of not loving the Pope. When, then, is love? Clearly many who sit in the pews have no idea. And even those who accept inerrancy and believe in the atonement often, perhaps usually, do not know.

With some diffidence and reserve because of the complex difficulties, I suggest the following: By loving in deed and truth we shall know that we are of the truth. And before him we shall persuade our heart that if it condemn us, that God is greater than our heart.

Westcott's objection of "decisive force" seems not to apply. He had said, "the conclusion is not one which flows naturally from the premise." Now, quite aside from Westcott's "whereinsoever," his premises and conclusion are less logical than ours. His interpretation is: "We shall assure our heart [of what?] because God is greater." How

could God's greatness, ipso facto and alone, assure us of his forgiveness? In fact, Westcott's final point (2) undermines his translation just
above. His translation was, "because God is greater." His final note is,
"Because we are in fellowship with God." For reasons such as these, I
have translated the phrases as, "We shall persuade our heart that God
is greater." This makes the second *oti* resumptive, but such seems to be
the lesser difficulty.

Undoubtedly many readers will judge the present interpretation to
be lacking. At any rate, it does not ignore the difficulties. If the reader
wishes to see a case of confusion of mind and an ignoring of the
problems, he may turn to Robert Cameron's *The First Epistle of John*,
chapter XI. Some readers may find all this complexity and analysis
not so much lacking as useless and tedious. Remember, however, that
we are dealing with God's Word, and that sincere devotion consists
not in the superficial reading of a chapter a day but in the very serious
consideration of what God meant. What some people call devotion is
simply a shirking of responsibility.

3:21.   Beloved, if our heart do not condemn us, we have boldness before God.

The last phrase of the preceding verse, "God knows all things," and
this verse, "if we have no qualms of conscience we have assurance"
seem to go without saying. Of course, God is omniscient; and, of
course, if we are not disturbed, we are confident. Why should John
make such obvious statements? The reason is that people need to be
reminded of what they ought not need to be reminded.

With respect to these two statements and also the next verse, the
commentators offer qualifications that bring the passage into accord
with common sense. The trouble is that the text does not state these
qualifications, and therefore they rest only on the authority of the
commentators. There is an annoying misprint in Stott's book at this
place. Misprints are the despair of every author. Stott quotes Westcott
as saying, "The thought here is of the boldness with which the Son
appears before the Father." Of course, Stott really meant no such
thing. Westcott wrote, "The thought here is of the boldness with
which the son [lower case] appears before the Father, and not that with
which the accused appears before the Judge." The present writer is

very sympathetic, for the printer of one of his volumes did not even use the corrections on the galley sheets. With the corrected galley sheets before him, he simply paginated them without the corrections.

3:22.   And what we ask, we receive from him, because we keep his commandments and do what is pleasing before him.

This verse may be properly regarded as completing the sentence begun in verse 21. Again, the commentators qualify what the text says: "If a prayer is to be answered, it must be according to his will." But, of course: if one prays that something take place which God has from eternity foreordained, it will take place. But many of us have prayed that communism be eradicated and that Christians be permitted to practice their religion without persecution or harassment. For 50 years we have so prayed, and the persecution is now more widespread than ever. F.F. Bruce slides over this difficulty by simply saying, "In such an atmosphere of love, confidence, and obedience it is the most natural thing in the world for the children to 'ask' their Father for what they need, assured that he will give them what they ask." But the Epistle does not say "ask for what they need." It says what or whatever we ask. A Christian in America does not *need* persecution to stop in Russia, China, and Uganda. But we pray for it.

If someone should try to alleviate the difficulty by saying that 50 years in God's sight is but a fraction of a second, and that God will grant our request later on—for Daniel and others prayed, and the return to Jerusalem came after 70 years—the answer is: our prayer is not that persecution should end in 70 years, or even in one year. We want an end to the sufferings and massacres now. Am I impatient? Well, do you want these outrages to continue?

It seems to me that the commentators are not completely honest on this point. Lenski says, "Scoffers challenge us to ask this or that folly which they propose and feel sure that we shall *not* get what we ask." But it is not a question of asking follies. It is not even a matter of personal advantage. We pray for the safety of missionaries, children, and natives. Then Idi Amin shoots down their plane and bludgeons the survivors to death. God has not given what we asked for. How then can A. W. Pink say, "It is certainly a strong assertion . . . altogether unqualified, absolute, and unrestricted." Of course, Pink can say this much. It is precisely in accord with the text. But then Pink continues, "We are on such terms with God that he will deny us nothing—that is the plain unequivocal meaning of what John says. And it is not to be modified or explained away by any supposed exceptions or reservations. It must be taken in all its breadth as literally true, in connection with the practice on which it is dependent. That practice is obedience."

Now, I am willing to admit that I am not so perfectly obedient to God's commands as to receive an affirmative answer to all my prayers, or any of them for that matter. But is there not some more devout Christian in the world who has prayed the same prayers? Were John's Christians in Asia Minor sufficiently obedient? Or did they not pray that persecution would end? Presumably they prayed that John would not be boiled in oil, or that Paul would not be beaten and stoned. But they did not receive what they asked for. To whom, then, does John's promise apply? I wonder if I could twist the Greek and make it read, "And if we ask, what we receive from him, we receive because we keep his commandments"? But the Greek scholars will shake their heads.

The remainder of the verse, beginning with the word *because*, is easy to exegete. The only difficulty is an unwarranted assumption that the doctrine of justification by faith alone is compromised. These words have to do with answers to prayer, not with justification. Neither our prayers nor our obedience are grounds for justification; but God has made obedience a ground for granting our requests. And the whole has as its background our assurance or boldness before him. Thus, there is no hint here of justification by obedience: it is answer to prayer by obedience.

> **3:23.   And this is his commandment, that we believe in the name of his son, Jesus Christ, and love one another, as he commanded us.**

This is probably the place where we should make a break in the outline and turn from love to faith. Some editors make the break at the end of the chapter. One cannot much object to this, for love and obedience still dominate verses 23 and 24. However, the changed subject, belief, comes in the present verse. Hence, our outline is,

C. Sonship Tested by Belief 3:23-4:6
  1. Belief in Christ is as much a commandment as love. 3:23 24
  2. The test of all spirits is the doctrine of the incarnation. 4:1-6

The widespread, so-called nondoctrinal Christianity, which puts great emphasis on experience, has a very narrow view of Christian experience. The worst of these people look upon the Ten Commandments as legalistic. A true, or at least a consistent, Christian regards obedience to commandments six, seven, and eight as genuine Christian experience. But where nondoctrinal pietism is rampant, where speaking in tongues is considered the acme of sanctification, where emotional upsets, confrontations, or encounters are recommended, the idea is absent that a study of the incarnation is Christian experience. And the idea that learning the Greek irregular verbs is a Christian experience never occurs to any of them. In fact, these people suggest and sometimes insist that a college student with a 3.5 grade point average cannot possibly be a good Christian. To be truly spiritual, a grade point average of 2.0 is the maximum. Just the other day, when the professor was trying to explain a point, a student rebuked him with, "You are too intellectual." One wonders why such students come to college at all. The reader should not dismiss any of this as exaggeration. Many chapel speakers warn the students against studying too much. But even if the warning were legitimate, it would be unnecessary. Hardly one student in a thousand studies too much.

Now, more positively, studying the doctrine of the incarnation is certainly Christian experience. At least, study is an experience; and if anyone studies theology for the purpose of increasing his faith, it is a Christian experience. There are many scriptural commands and exhortations to meditate on God's law day and night. God requires of us daily exegesis, for "this is his commandment, that we believe in the name of his Son."

How can we obey this commandment? First, we must exegete it and understand it. Is it not obvious that it does not mean to believe that there was once a man named Jesus? In Latin American Catholicism there are many boys superstitiously, if not blasphemously, named Jesus. No Christian could ever give his son that name. Even so, what does believing in his name mean? Westcott says, and I quote with approval, "It is equivalent to 'believe as true the message which the name conveys.' " And the name conveys the full message of the New Testament. Paul asserted his innocence of the blood of all men on the ground that he had preached the whole counsel of God. But most fundamentalist pastors preach only a fraction, and the experiential, pietistic churches preach even a smaller fraction. Let the reader ask himself: When have I last heard a sermon on the incarnation? Perhaps last Christmas? And did that sermon cover more than a few of the outstanding circumstances? Of course, a single sermon cannot cover everything. But that is just the reason why there should be sermons on the incarnation at times in addition to Christmas. Undoubtedly we should love one another. But obedience to one commandment does not excuse disobedience to another one. Belief and love are both required. And without the belief, love remains uninformed.

Having so emphasized the need of serious study and meditation, the present writer is obliged, not indeed to explain the whole counsel of God in this chapter, but at least to bring forth so much of that counsel as he can see in this verse.

The usual translation of the middle phrase of the verse is, "believe on, or in, the name of his Son." The reason is that the dative case in Greek, without any preposition, ordinarily requires the preposition *in, to,* or *by,* in English. Sometimes even English omits the preposition; for example, I pray to God, or I pray God; or even, "I gave him the book," instead of "I gave the book to him." Or again, in the sentence "every man labors for himself," the word *himself* in Greek is a dative without any preposition.

Now, in Greek the verb *pisteuō, believe,* may take an object either in the accusative or the dative. In English the object, if a noun and not a clause, must be accusative because English has no dative. But those who know German realize that if a person is drowning, he should call, *Helfen Sie mir;* not *helfen Sie mich.* Of course, though you made a grammatical mistake, they would probably pull you out of the water anyway. Now, I Corinthians 13:7 says, "Love believes all things." The "all things" is an accusative pronoun. But in Luke 1:20 we have a simple dative: "You did not believe my words." Similarly John 2:22, "They believed the writing and the word." Hence, if anyone tries to extend the meaning of our present verse by insisting on the English preposition *in,* and interprets it as something other than the simple object of belief, as if believing in a person were different from believing what the person says, he misunderstands what John wrote.

All this Greek may bore some who read these pages; but the same point will later come up most interestingly in I John 5:10. This verse begins with *pisteuein eis. Eis* is the preposition *into*. "He who believes into the Son of God." Then comes the simple dative: "He who does not believe God." Then third, "he has not believed into the witness which God witnessed." Obviously the witness, the testimony, or the record as King James has it, is not a person, even though preceded by *eis*. The conclusion is that prepositions do not distinguish belief *in* a person from belief *that* a proposition is true. There are not several types of believing, though there are many different objects of belief.

Sometimes supposedly pious theories of differences in believing become more complicated than the Greek grammar. Though I dislike a certain overtone in Lenski's paragraph (p. 480), he is completely correct when he says, "Some offer these distinctions in meaning: *pisteuein tini* is *assensus*, (so here); *pisteuein tina* is *notitio; pisteuein eis* is *fiducia*. These distinctions are specious." They certainly are. No matter whether this verb is followed by a dative, an accusative, or a clause, it means simply *believe*. Belief is the voluntary assent to an understood proposition; and when we say we believe a man, or believe in a man, we mean we accept as true what he says. Hence, when we believe Jesus' name, we mean we believe what he said.

Stott notes that the verb *believe* is aorist (actually aorist subjunctive), and that the verb *love* is in the present tense. On this ground he seems to suggest that belief is a single act in past time and love is a continuing attitude. Does he mean that we no longer believe? Ask some friendly Greek professor whether or not an aorist subjunctive can have a present sense. Acts 25:13 has an aorist participle that is future to the main verb. Naturally, believing is a present and a continuing mental activity, quite as much as loving.

3:24.   And he who keeps his commandments remains in him and he in him. And by this we know that he remains in us, from the Spirit whom he gave us.

Belief as well as love are both commandments. There are also commandments, both positive and negative, relative to congregational worship. Certain types of prayer are enjoined and other types forbidden. He who obeys these abides in Christ and Christ in him. The idea of the indwelling Christ and our indwelling him is a theme mystics love to dilate upon. What they say is often unintelligible. The origin of Christian mysticism is probably Dionysius the Areopagite: not Paul's Athenian convert, but a fifth century author who took his name. Even Thomas Aquinas thought the books came from Paul's convert. This ignorance enhanced the fortunes of mysticism in Christendom. I shall quote a few lines and the reader may judge as to its intelligibility.

> Triad supernal, both super-God and super-good, Guardian of the theosophy of Christian men, direct us aright to the super-unknown and super-brilliant and highest summit of the mystic oracles, where the simple and absolute and changeless mysteries of theology lie hidden within the super-luminous gloom of the silence, revealing hidden things, which in its deepest darkness shines above the most super-brilliant, and in the altogether impalpable and invisible fills to overflowing the eyeless minds with glory of surpassing beauty. (*Mystic Theology* 1:1)

All in one sentence, too!

Now, the New Testament does indeed teach a mutual indwelling of Christ and the believer. There is a very real sense in which minds interpenetrate. In I Corinthians 2:16 Paul asserts that "we have the mind of Christ."[1] Christ dwells in us and we in him by our thinking and believing his doctrines. As John says in his Gospel 8:51, "He who maintains my doctrine shall not see death, ever." This is intelligible. Mysticism and pietism are not.

Neither Bruce nor Stott explains what "abiding" is. However, Stott makes a commendable remark:

> Abiding in Christ is not a mystical experience which any man may claim; [I hope this does not mean that it is a mystical experience some men may claim.] its indispensable accompaniments are the confession of Jesus as the Son of God come in the flesh, and a consistent life of holiness and love. . . . It may at first sight seem that this reference to the Holy Spirit [the last phrase of the verse] within us introduces a subjective criterion of assurance (like Rom. 8:15, 16) which is inconsistent with what has gone before.

---

[1]Compare my Commentary on *I Corinthians.*

Now, I do not believe that Romans introduces a subjective criterion; and I certainly reject the idea that Paul in Romans is in any way inconsistent with John. But Stott's rejection of mysticism and his emphasis on belief in the incarnation is most commendable.

What, then, about the Holy Spirit? The verse says that our knowledge of abiding in Christ comes from the Spirit. There seems to be just one explanation. Faith or belief, and repentance, are the gift of God. The man dead in sin cannot even prepare himself for conversion. He must first be regenerated or raised from the dead by the Spirit. He whose will is alienated from God and resists the gospel must be made willing; and it is the Spirit who does so.

Thus we may paraphrase the verse as, "By keeping his commandments our knowledge of abiding in him comes from the Holy Spirit."

This is the end of chapter 3.

The Fourth Chapter

SOME outlines make a sharp break at this point. We have seen that the new subject matter was introduced in 3:23. That the paragraph continues through 4:6 is generally agreed upon, even though the connection between 4:6 and 4:7 is disputed.

> **4:1.   Beloved, do not believe every spirit; but evaluate the spirits [to see] if they are of God, because many false prophets have come into the world.**

Here the object of the verb *believe* is a simple dative, without a preposition. John tells us not to believe every religious preacher. Many do not preach the truth.

There was a certain "Christian college" whose faculty, students, and trustees were exceedingly evangelistic. In fact, the trustees thought that "evangelical" meant the forceful evangelistic methods of which they approved. At a certain juncture a few of this community asked, "Why does the college largely oppose Jehovah's Witnesses? They are evangelistic!" John's reply is: analyze the theology and distinguish between truth and falsehood; evaluate the preachers, do not believe everything you hear. But those college people were not much interested in believing anything: they wanted fervent oratory, rousing songs, and an emotional experience. Analysis and evaluation are such cold, intellectual concepts! But this sort of religion has a frightful misconception of the nature of God. God is truth, not emotion. Let those who want emotion and experience apply to the whirling dervishes. Those sources will not contaminate them by any truth.

The spirits whom John has in mind are not the demons and satanic angels, though Satan no doubt inspires them; but rather these spirits are men, preachers, religious leaders of whatever sort, who teach error. Note now that the Epistle as a whole and this verse in particular are addressed to the brethren; namely, to every Christian. The fact that faithful pastors and orthodox professors are better able to evaluate does not excuse those in the pews from doing their own evaluating. Millions of people depend on the Pope to do their judging for them. The Roman church thinks of the Scripture as addressed to the bishops; and since 1870 an ex cathedra papal encyclical settles any matter. In the secular world today there is something similar. The latest scientific theory is uncritically accepted by the populace and the government, so that atheistic evolution must be taught in the schools and the teaching of creationism is the establishment of religion. The conscientious and informed Christian rejects the Pope and HEW as well. The attempt to close Christian schools in Ohio, and the sentence of imprisonment of Christian parents in Kentucky, and the constant harassment of Christian colleges by HEW, should convince myopic pietists who divorce theory from practice that nothing is more practical than theory. The defense of Christian institutions against socialistic government is a theological battle. Judge the spirits. What about a president who claims to be born again and appoints a hydrophobic female abortionist to administer the federal abortion system? We should judge the spirits. Abortion is not of God.

There were many false prophets in John's day, and no fewer now. The world is full of them. Those instanced in the previous paragraph are not all by any means.

4:2. By this know the spirit of God: every spirit who confesses Jesus Christ come in the flesh is of God.

The translation: The verb form *know* is either indicative or imperative. The imperative seems to fit the context better because the people have not yet judged these false prophets. John commands them to do so in verse 1, and gives them the criterion in verse 2. If an indicative were needed, it would be future: 'Judge . . . by this you will know.'

The criterion of judgment is the spirits' confession of the incarnate Christ. It is not best to say "who confesses that Jesus Christ has come in the flesh." There is a difference in meaning and emphasis. If one say "confesses that Jesus Christ has come in the flesh," the emphasis is on the incarnation as such. Of course, this is important and essential. But the present phrase both includes and extends beyond it. It is a confession of Christ. The emphasis is on Christ, and not simply on one facet of Christ's function. For example, the participle "having come" is adjectival and suggests, with the help of other passages, that Christ was preexistent. No doubt we can say that John Jones came in the flesh on the day of his birth; but this would be a strange expression. When we say "Christ come in the flesh," it is not a strange expression, and it does not mean simply that he was born on a certain day in 6 B.C. Hence, while the verse surely applies to Docetics, Gnostics or otherwise, its application is wider. It applies to anyone who denies Christ—the Christ who came, died, and rose again.

In view of the fact that everybody is inconsistent to some degree, the importance of the interpretation becomes clearer. Someone could assert a true incarnation, a true incarnation of a heavenly being, and deny many other doctrines. Arius did so. Jehovah's Witnesses do so. My wife and I accepted one of her college chums' invitation to dinner. The parents of the girl were old fashioned Russellites. The father said grace in the name of "Jesus, our Redeemer." But he believed that the redeemer was a created angel. Therefore, we see that belief in a non-docetic incarnation alone is not satisfactory. We must test prophets on many points, not just one or two.

4:3a.   And every spirit who does not confess Jesus is not of God.

The translation: There is a definite article before the name Jesus: *the* Jesus. This could be strengthened to "*this* Jesus," the one mentioned as having come. But as the article is weaker than the demonstrative, this interpretation cannot be insisted upon.

The verse as a whole is the negative assertion of the positive in the preceding verse. All who confess Jesus are of God; all who do not are not of God. These two do not form an inference; they form a conjunction. It is not valid to argue, All who confess Jesus are of God, *therefore* all who do not are not of God. This reasoning is fallacious because "all Boston terriers are dogs" does not imply that "all who are not Boston terriers are not dogs." John is not guilty of such an elementary logical blunder. He is stating a conjunction. All who confess are and—the conjunction *and*—all who do not, are not. It is the same as: all who vote for Democratic candidates are honest, and all who do not are not honest. These two statements are not inconsistent; but the second does not follow from the first. Nor does it follow that the apostle was a Democrat.

There is another point here that reveals the unchristian, or unwittingly anti-Christian views of some, at least a few, contemporaries. Nearly everyone has heard religious and other leaders urge people to emphasize the positive and not to be so negative. Positive is good; negative is bad. This is both anti-Christian and illogical. There can be no positive without a negative. If positively all Calvinists are Reformed, we must assert negatively that no Calvinist is Arminian. If we say positively that some books are interesting, we must contradict those students who say no books are. Christians must assert many negatives. We say adultery is never right, heresy is not truth, Zen is not good. The Bible is full of negatives. Therefore, those who repudiate negative thinking repudiate Christian thinking. In fact, they do not think; at least they do not think logically, for there is no positive without its complementary negative. And even aside from the law of contradiction, and contraposition, John asserts other negatives.

4:3b.   And this is the [spirit] of the Antichrist, which you heard is coming, and now is already in the world.

The translation: The neuter noun *spirit* obviously must be inserted in the translation. Even the Holy Spirit is neuter in Greek, for unlike English, Greek and most other languages do not have natural gender. The relative pronoun *which,* because clearly neuter, has as its antecedent *spirit* and not *Antichrist.*

In the first half of the verse and in the preceding verses John was speaking of individual persons: false prophets, several antichrists, and The Antichrist. But there is a shift in his meaning here. Here the inserted word *spirit* does not designate an individual person. The phrase "the spirit of the Antichrist" is like "the spirit of '76," or "the spirit of the times." It means attitude, mind-set, a complex of ideas. Such again will be the obvious meaning at the end of 4:6. This produces an awkwardness in the present verse. Strictly speaking the people had not heard that a certain "Zeitgeist" was coming. This was new information, first given to them in 2:18. What they had heard was that in the last time the Antichrist would come. Hence, in sense, though not in grammar, we should understand: this is the mind-set of the Antichrist, whom you heard is coming, and it, this mind-set, is already in the world.

It is in this connection that Bultmann claims John as a forerunner of his own theology. He stresses the fact that the relative pronoun is neuter and not masculine. The Antichrist, therefore, is not pictured as a concrete figure. The author (not really John) alludes to the prophecy of mythological apocalyptic, as in 2:18. This prophecy is here demythologized by reducing the Antichrist to the historical false prophets. The mythology has been fulfilled in them, and no future mythological Antichrist is in view.

Even if my interpretation is wrong, still Bultmann's demythologization is too heavy to hang on a neuter relative.

There is no inconsistency between saying that the attitude of the Antichrist is now in the world and also saying that the personal Antichrist will come later on. It is application, not demythologization, when we conclude that the preaching of the false prophets today is controlled, like the preaching of their predecessors, by the principles, ideas, and purposes of the Antichrist. But when we do so, and suggest that the National Council and World Council, financing terrorism, are controlled by Satan, we are looked down upon as being uncivilized and impolite. Contemporary religion has advanced far beyond the crudities of the apostles. These fundamentalists are simply hopeless.

However, the crude apostle continues:

4:4   You are of God, [my] children, and you have conquered them, because greater is he in you than he in the world.

Would it not be wonderful if what John said were true! But the false prophets have conquered. They have captured the major denominations; they control the press so that we are constantly misrepresented and ridiculed. And so on and so on. Did not Christ himself prophesy that when he returns he will find no, or little, faith among the populace?

Yet, John's words are indeed true. We children of John have conquered the false prophets. They failed to convince us of Wellhausen's higher criticism. They failed to convince us that there was no Hittite nation. They failed to convince us that the Pentateuch was written after the Babylonian captivity. We still believe in the virgin birth, the atonement, and the resurrection. We have conquered them. They could not conquer us.

The reason is that they are controlled by the Antichrist, but Christ in us is greater. This leads us into the next verse.

4:5. They are of the world. Therefore they speak from a worldly point of view, and the world hears them.

The translation: Of course, the middle phrase is literally "They speak of, from, out of, the world."

The reason for the widespread apostasy in Christendom is that the people and the false prophets have the same inclinations. When the latter emphasize the dignity of man and attack total depravity, the people are gratified. In spite of the corruption in government, the violence of labor unions, embezzlement and fraud in business, people like to think "I'm all right, you're all right." When the churches subsidize labor unions for prostitutes and encourage homosexuals, they seem to proclaim liberty throughout the land. This panders to the desire for individual autonomy. Auto-nomy means, each one is a law to himself. And with complete inconsistency these are the people who encourage bureaucratic socialism. But, of course, they expect the bureaucracy to pay for their abortions. This gives them greater sexual freedom. When religious leaders speak from a worldly point of view, naturally the world hears them.

4:6. [But] we are of God. He who knows God hears us. He who is not of God does not hear us. By this we know the spirit of truth and the spirit of error.

As in John's day, so, too, today, non-Christian religious leaders claim to know God. Every book on the philosophy of religion has a theology. What the author thinks about God governs his analyses and constructions. If, as is usual today, he justifies his ideas of God by his own religious experience, he is merely asserting his theories on his own authority. If, as in an earlier time, he claims to know God by examining the universe and producing a cosmological argument, it can be shown that his inferences are invalid. Man's only way of knowing God is by the reception of theological information verbally revealed to him. The reception, that is, the assent to or belief in the doctrines revealed is the work of God, for faith or belief is a divinely given gift. Those to whom God has not given this gift do not "hear" us. Of course, they hear the words we speak; they may with some attention understand what we say; but they believe it false. We have the spirit of truth; they have the spirit of error.

Although regeneration is the work of the Holy Spirit, and although he may be called the Spirit of Truth, the two phrases here seem to indicate the true and the false opinions, or mind-sets, of the opposing parties. It is not that the Christian directly perceives the devil or even an antichrist, but rather that he perceives the falsity of the false prophet's religion and infers that he speaks from the devil. We may read a book or hear a lecture, and at the beginning have no knowledge of the author's position. Then as he proceeds we come to see that his words are pervaded by the spirit of error.

Some Christians do not grasp this very easily or very soon. False prophets are often persuasive and deceptive. They use evangelical terms, but are not evangelicals. They talk about the authority of the Bible yet their notion of authority permits the Bible to contain any number of errors. And thus they subvert seminaries, denominations, and simple Christians. The only protection the latter can have is a more extensive knowledge—a knowledge of God and a knowledge of the wiles of the devil. The so-called neoorthodox may say, and some have said, "I believe in the resurrection of Christ; it is an actual event; it is essential to Christianity." But then in the fine print you discover that for them the word *resurrection* means any putative Christian's experience of encounter or confrontation. Of course, the resurrection is an actual event; it takes place just once—once for each individual. But it is not the event of Jesus' coming out of the tomb on a particular Sunday in a definite year a long time ago. Let it be pointedly stated that "on the third day he rose again." It is not merely a dated event: it is that particular date.

If, however, we know God, that is, the information he has revealed, and if we understand what the false prophet is saying, we ipso facto distinguish between the spirit of truth and the spirit of error.

There is one detail that the previous paragraph does not make clear. In 4:4 John says "you are of God." He is speaking of his followers, and by inference of us today. But 4:6 begins "We are of God." Again by inference this applies to present-day pastors. But the immediate reference is to John himself, plus perhaps the other apostles, and even their assistants. In this verse the contrast is between two groups of religious leaders: the apostles and the false prophets. Paul, too, you will remember, had to defend his apostolic authority in order to enforce his doctrine against a perverted preaching. *"We* are of God; and anyone who knows God hears *us."* Applications of John's message to our present predicaments are to be encouraged; but a realization of the apostles' own difficulties, far from detracting from the application, considerably enforces it.

One commentator, whose name need not be mentioned, completely misunderstands this verse, with the result that his comments are a confused mixture of truth and error. He writes, "The spirit of error is abroad. . . . How are you to be prepared? Let me warn you that it is not head knowledge that will do; not logic, or rhetoric, or philosophy, or theology; not creeds, or catechisms, or confessions; . . . no, nothing will do but God being in you."

Now first, it is true that skill in rhetoric will protect no one from error. Nor will some philosophy. A detailed knowledge of Aristotle or of Kant is of help only in the sense that such study exercises our ability to analyze. Or, to put it into other words, a study of philosophy discovers to us what the main problems of knowledge are and what the range of possible solutions is. We learn the implications of plausible principles; and by all this we are better able to avoid error. The systems themselves—Aristotelianism, Hegelianism, and surely Dewey's Instrumentalism—are useless as bases on which to take our stand. Yet studying them is the very best way of developing our innate logical ability. Without logic we cannot distinguish between a valid and an invalid syllogism. It is necessary so to distinguish because false prophets often quote Scripture and then invalidly deduce false conclusions. A knowledge of logic as well as a knowledge of theology is presumably "head knowledge." Is there any other kind of knowledge? How can there be knowledge without consciousness? Of course, the word "head" is wrong-headed, for two reasons. First, the head or brain is a corporeal organ; and Christians are not behaviorists. Thinking is a function of the mind, not of the brain or muscles, as John Dewey claims. Then, second, if this reference to head knowledge is meant to suggest a contrast with heart knowledge, the whole is unscriptural, for the Old Testament uses the term *heart* as a metaphorical term for the mind. In Old Testament language it is the heart that knows, thinks, calculates, either good or evil.

Then further, contrary to what the commentator wrote, it is indeed theology, creeds, and catechisms that protect us from error. Not all creeds and catechisms do so. It is those documents which are founded upon and validly deduced from Scripture. If we state what we believe, in our own words, without limiting ourselves to verbatim quotations from Scripture, we are talking theology. Every sermon preached is theology, good or bad. The Westminster Confession and Catechisms were formulated by careful Christian scholars. They give the best summary of the biblical system ever published. A knowledge of them is the very best way to distinguish false prophets from true. This is not to say that we should not study the Bible itself. Nor is it to say that this confession and these catechisms are inerrant. But they are more likely to be the truth than any other book or sermon. They summarize the Bible; and if we know their contents, we much more easily escape being deceived.

Now, finally, the commentator rejects all these and depends on "God being in you." But he nowhere explains what "God being in you" means. Are we to throw away our volumes on systematic theology, and the Bible as well, and wait for a special extra-biblical revelation direct from God? I reply that we are neither mystics nor apostles. It is in the Scripture that God speaks to us, has spoken to us; and the Scripture is not only profitable for doctrine but is alone sufficient to make a man of God *thoroughly* furnished to *all* good works. If God is in us, it is because we keep the Scripture in mind.

> **4:7.   Beloved, let us love each other because love is of God, and everyone who loves has been born of God and knows God.**

Here, according to our defective outline, a new section begins. Defective as ours is, virtually all outlines make a break at this verse. The disagreement concerns whether the break is major or subsidiary. This outline makes it a major break.

III. Closer Correlation of Righteousness, Love, and Belief   4:7-5:21
   A. Love and Belief   4:7-5:3
     1. God is Love (love, a condition of fellowship because of God's nature and the resulting obligations).   7-12

The exhortation to love one another is based on the statement that love is of God. The remainder of the verse is rather an additional idea. Lenski stresses the article before the noun *love,* makes it a demonstrative, and translates it as "this love is from God." I am not impressed with Lenski's grammar, for abstract nouns usually take the article. However, his reasons and understanding are excellent. John is not saying that all sorts of emotions called love are from God. The romanticism of Goethe, and much more the present sexual debauchery, are not from God. John certainly means (this) Christian love. It is not an emotion. Unlike sporadic ecstasies and hectic palpitations, this love is a settled decision to obey God's laws.

Surely it is false to say that everyone who experiences emotional highs is born of God. But everyone who exhibits Chrisian love knows God, for only by knowing God can our conduct be Christian. If we do not know what God requires of us in connection with our fellow Christians, we just would not know how we ought to act. This last half of the verse is neither the premise nor the conclusion of the exhortation. At our first reading, we might expect to find "Let us love each other because love is of God and everyone born of God loves." This would produce an implication: Since love is of God, and since everyone born of God loves, let us discharge our obligation and love our fellow Christians. But this is exactly the reverse of what John wrote. Still less is the exhortation a premise, as if it were "Let us love, therefore everyone born of God loves." The whole verse, accordingly, must be taken as a conjunction with *kai* (and); and it is the reverse of our first expectation: Let us love because love is of God and everyone who loves is born of God. Not: "everyone born of God loves."

This makes it clear that John does not have romantic emotions in mind. While *ãgapao* can mean sexual love, here it means Christian

love. The word *love* in any language has several meanings. Though
Lenski's grammar at this point may be substandard, I am happy to
quote with approval and emphasis this fine passage: "*Agapē* is defined
as the love of intelligence, of *comprehension* and understanding. It
always has that meaning in the New Testament, most completely so
here where it speaks of God's love. Combined with this is *purpose,* a
purpose that corresponds to the comprehension of the object. . . .
Saving *agapē* thus accompanies *charis, eleos,* compassion, benevo-
lence" (p. 499).

**4:8.   He who does not love does not know God, because
God is love.**

This is the verse which Mary Baker Eddy made the basis of Christian
Science. Joseph Fletcher might have done so, too, if he had had as
much respect for the Scripture as Mary Baker Eddy had. Both examples
show how sadly love can be misinterpreted. Some more orthodox
writers have regarded the final phrase as a definition of God. This has
a more pious sound; but note that John also says, "God is spirit";
"God is Light"; and Christ said, "I am the Truth." The Holy Spirit is
"the Spirit of Truth." None of these is precisely a definition. The term
spirit designates God's essence, the nature of his being, the "matter"
or "substance" of which he is composed. Of course, God is not
"composed." He is simple. He may be pure Form, but he has no
Aristotelian Matter, nor the matter of contemporary common opinion.
He is spirit, not body. The term *spirit,* however, all by itself does not
distinguish God from other spirits, ourselves for example, and hence,
is not a definition. Similarly, it is no definition to say God is *Light,* for
light is metaphorical and must be reduced to literal language. It is
generally supposed to denote knowledge and righteousness. Since the
blessed angels are perfectly righteous, this term, too, by itself, does not
define God. One would have to add that God is the source of all
righteousness. This the angels are not. Probably *Truth* comes nearest
to being a definition, for while mankind knows a little truth, a few
true propositions, God is Truth itself and is omniscient. The phrase
"God, who is truth itself" comes from the Westminster Confession,
I, iv.

Some readers are probably puzzled as to why this commentary seems to deprecate love and emphasize truth. The answer is obvious. In all ages, and never so much as now, love is misunderstood, not only by the filthy homosexuals whose activities make ordinary whoremongering seem almost righteous; but particularly by the religious leaders who want to accept homosexuals as members in good standing—and not only so, but even want to ordain them as ministers, no less. This is not all. Many good devout people, who view contemporary depravity with horror, nevertheless have been contaminated by romanticism, emotionalism, and experiences of titillation and excitement. Very few people misunderstand truth. Humanistic philosophers, indeed, relativists, of whom there are too many, and instrumentalists, have a wrong conception of truth. When speaking to them we must say, fixed truth, absolute truth, or something to that effect. Yet by their opposition to unchanging truth, they show that they know what the word *truth* ordinarily means. The remainder of the public do not need these adjectives. Therefore, while love is almost universally misunderstood, truth is not.

Now, in this verse, it says that God is love. What this love is will be explained in the next few verses, and it is totally unlike Mrs. Eddy's and Dr. Fletcher's concepts.

4:9.   By this the love of God in us is made clear in that God sent his only Son into the world in order that we might live through him.

This is not so difficult a verse as many others, but it has several points that need pointing out. First, the words "in us" are puzzling and the commentators make various guesses. The King James translation makes very good sense in itself, and its phrase "toward us" fits in perfectly with the second half of the verse. Unfortunately, the Greek preposition can hardly mean "toward." RSV and NIV translate it "among us." This is almost unintelligible: do they mean that Christ lived in Palestine among his people? Such an interpretation is otiose. If we should translate the words literally, "in us," and suppose that this love is the love that God engenders in our heart, the two parts of the verse would not fit together. Consider: our subjective love of God is made clear (to our neighbors?) because God sent his Son. The sense of the KJV must be preserved, and if a better translation be necessary, let it read, "The love of God in our case." What God's love really is, is clarified by the fact that he sent his Son to redeem us. This keeps the two parts of the verse together, as it also gives the explanation needed to complete the previous two verses. Love, in God, consists in sending his Son to redeem the elect. How different from Fletcher's love!

The next point in the verse is the word *monogenē*. We are accustomed to the translation "only-begotten." This is not really a good translation. *Mono-genēs* means "one of a kind." The French translation is "Fils unique." But when a certain theologian tried to rule out the doctrine of the eternal generation of the Son, he went too far. It is true that *gignomai* (become) and *gennaō* (beget) are two different verbs. It is also true that *genos* means a class or kind. "Fils unique" is a very good translation. Yet *genos* also means descent from a common ancestor, and the two verbs come from the same root. At any rate, though we translate *monogenēs* as *unique,* the doctrine of eternal generation and the verb *gennaō* are found in Hebrews 1:5.

The second half of the verse now gives us the purpose, or a part of the purpose, of our Savior's first advent. John does not, cannot, put all the doctrine of the atonement in this verse. The full doctrine, as formulated in the Westminster Confession, is obtained by combining and summarizing many scriptural passages. We should not demand that every sermon without exception should restrict itself to the atonement; but we should expect that the atonement be the center of all preaching. The atonement is not the basis of Christianity. The Trinity is more fundamental. The atonement is central. Here the purpose of God's sending his Son is that we should have life in him. We were dead in sin, and God, on account of Christ, resurrects us to newness of life.

We note, too, that while the atonement is central, this verse bears on the doctrine of the Trinity. God sent his Son. Christ did not come of his own individual volition. He was sent. This does not mean that he was unwilling and reluctant to come. In fact, the phrase "his own individual volition" is very poor theology. The three Persons of the Trinity have but one will. On earth Christ did not act on his own volition: "I did not come of myself (on my own authority), but he who sent me is true"; and, "I do nothing on my own authority, but as the Father has taught me, these things I speak" (the Gospel 7:28; 8:28, 42). There is, then, here some information about the intertrinitarian relationships: the Father sent the Son. And though the atonement is central, it could not be true if it were not founded on the doctrine of the Trinity. In our present age we must preach this doctrine and all the more is it necessary because so few of even the well-meaning pastors preach it.

4:10.   In this is love: not that we loved God, but that he himself loved us and sent his Son [to be] a propitiation for our sins.

The two instances of the verb *love* are different in tense, a difference which permits a trifle more clarity than English does. The first instance, "not that we loved God" is in the perfect tense. We do not really push the Greek too far when we say, "Not that we began in the past to love God and continue now to do so." The second instance, "he himself loved us"—and we note in passing the emphatic *himself*—is in the aorist tense, designating a particular point in past time. The particular point need not be literally 60 seconds, but can refer to an extended period of time regarded as a unit. For example, particularly because it is so far in the past, we can say, "Athens and Sparta fought the Peloponnesian War." It was a 30-year war, but we look on it as one event. So here, God sent his Son to be a propitiation. The sending could refer to the virgin birth; the propitiation, of course, refers to his death; but the whole 30 years is regarded as a unit. This condensation of time adds emphasis: it confronts us with the purpose of Christ's activity as a whole, rather than dispersing our attention through a multiplicity of details.

The ideas of this verse have already been commented on. The greatest instance of love rules out a Freudian or even a romantic definition: Joseph Fletcher is here denounced. So are all others who wish to avoid the ideas of wrath, penalty, and propitiation. It is a disgrace that the NIV, with its many excellencies, and with its claim to loyalty to the Scriptures as the RSV cannot claim, here in this verse and its parallels eliminates the idea of propitiation by substituting an ambiguous phrase.

There are all sorts of atonements and all sorts of sacrifices. There is the sacrifice bunt in baseball. Two hot-headed athletes can be *at one* again by agreeing to forget their quarrel. The song "God Bless America" contains the phrase, "The light from above." This is vague enough to mean almost anything. It could even refer to Seurat and his pointillism, at least if he had been an American instead of French. The large group of independent churches today, those who will have no dealings with the National Council, are themselves debilitated by vagueness. Yes, they may be clear on a few things; but contemporary phraseology constantly replaces accurate terminology with pious platitudes. Then in the course of a generation the original meaning is forgotten and a surface sheen camouflages the inner emptiness.

Christ came to die as a propitiation of the righteous wrath of his Father. he suffered the penalty of sin instead of our suffering it. He bore our sins in his own body on the tree, and by his stripes we are healed. This is what love is.

> **4:11.   Beloved, if God thus loved us, we also ought to love each other.**

No further comment is needed.

> **4:12.   No one has ever seen God. If we love each other, God remains in us and his love is made complete in us.**

It is hard to be sure why John began this verse with the statement that no one has ever seen God. The statement itself is true, and is found many times in the Scripture. Abraham did not see God when the three persons visited him. It was a theophany; it was God in disguise. Moses did not see God. And the Gospel 1:18 says, "No one has ever seen God." In the Gospel this statement fits the context. It forms a contrast with "the only God who is in the bosom of the Father has explained him." But here in the Epistle, the statement does not seem to fit the context.

Yet, if we meditate on the verse, a possible interpretation comes to mind. God is invisible because he is spirit and not body. For many people this puts a great distance between him and us. Men are so bogged down in sensation that spiritual realities seem unreal. Because of this John wishes to reassure us that there is no "distance" between us and God. Like our thoughts, God is both unseen and really present.

This connection between God and ourselves can be expressed in two ways. Paul said, "In him we live and move and have our being." This includes all men, not just Christians. But also for us Christians, God lives in us. The evidence that God is in us, and not far away, is that we love other Christians.

A few readers may be puzzled by the last phrase of the verse: God's love is completed or perfected in us. Is not God's love perfect in itself? Can God develop from a less complete to a more complete status? Scripture has two or three other instances where it could seem that God is incomplete and that Paul "must fill up that which is behind of the afflictions of Christ in my flesh" (Col. 1:24). Even the commentators often regard the sense of our verse as something startling. Its meaning, however, seems quite simple: one of the aims of God's love, after Christ's death on the cross, is to produce our love of him and of the brethren. His purpose, therefore, is so far fulfilled when we have this love. Of course, there are still further purposes yet to be fulfilled, but this one, our love, helps to complete God's purposes.

4:13.   By this we know that we remain in him and he in us, because he has given us [a share] of his Spirit.

Our outline regards this as the start of a slightly subordinate paragraph. With the help of verse 16, we may say that another obligation love places upon us is to believe that Jesus is the Son of God.

This main specification is introduced by asserting that the gift of the Holy Spirit to us assures us that we live in God and he lives in us.

Lenski is a little disturbed at Robertson's grammatical statement that *ek* is partitive: God gave us a part of his Spirit. "Since when is the Holy Spirit divided into parts?" Lenski exclaims. But probably Robertson meant no more than Lenski means in his perfectly satisfactory interpretation. God has given us some gifts from his Spirit. God does not so give the indivisible Spirit to one human being that every other is prevented from having him, too. God gave the Spirit at Pentecost; but the gift was the ability to speak in foreign languages. God gives us his Spirit when he gives us the volition of love. The particular gift is always only a part of what the Spirit can do; but we can still say that God gives us his Spirit. Now, what gift does John particularly have in mind here?

4:14.   And we have beheld and we testify that the Father sent his Son as Savior of the world.

The translation: The subject pronoun *we* is explicit, as it is usually not in Greek. It is therefore emphatic. This permits the following interpretation.

Although John often uses *we* to include his "children," and all later Christians, here it seems that he has in mind the apostles alone. The verb *tetheametha,* see, behold, contemplate, can certainly refer to the disciples' walking around Palestine with Jesus. Then, too, there is a verbal reference back to verse 12: No man has ever seen God, but we have seen. . . ." If John intended this contrast, the present verse must refer to the disciples alone.

Now, there is a certain awkwardness of condensation in the verse. Expanded it would read, We contemplated Jesus 50 years ago and were convinced and now testify that the Father sent him as Savior of the world.

The verb *tetheametha* can refer to visual sensation, but usually it emphasizes a different idea. It means to behold something extraordinary, striking, an astounding or fearful spectacle. The idea of wonder, steady contemplation, awe, and sometimes fear, is prominent. The visual sensation or perception of the disciples was that of a man, dressed in the usual clothing, walking around, and doing this and that. Some of this and that was miraculous. They wondered, they pondered, and they concluded that this man was the Son of God, whose Father had sent him to be the Savior of the world. This conclusion is nothing that can be deduced from sensory experience. It was a revelation from the Father himself, by his Spirit. It is to this that John and the other disciples testify.

This, I believe, is the correct interpretation; but there is a difficulty which should not be concealed from the English reader. The verb in this verse is the same as in 4:12. There it meant visual sensation. Here it cannot. The verb in the Gospel is a different verb for *see.* This latter verb *oraō* mostly means eyesight, or sight in a dream; but it also, infrequently, means *contemplate*. The verb in 4:12, 14 has the proportion reversed: *contemplate* is the main meaning, but it can also be used for eyesight. One can only guess why John used the same verb in different senses only two verses apart. Westcott's attempt seems weak; he says that "strictly speaking the immediate objects of *tetheametha* and *marturoumen* [testify] are different. The object of contemplation was the revelation of the Lord's Life: the object of witness, the declaration of its meaning." Yet Westcott himself adds, only a few lines below, "His Life was the object of contemplation (*theasthai*) and not of vision." His reference to the verb in 4:12 leaves his total view in confusion.

4:15.   If anyone confess that Jesus is the Son of God, God dwells in him and he in God.

There are serious difficulties in this and similar verses which most commentators are pleased to ignore. Perhaps they think the solution is too obvious to mention. But two solutions compete for acceptance, an easy or loose one, and a difficult or strict one.

Let us first state the difficulty. Does this verse mean that everyone who confesses that Jesus is the Son of God is without question elect and regenerate? Arius and Jehovah's Witnesses so confess, but the long so-called Athanasian—not Nicene—Creed damns them. Philo was a Jew and had never heard of Jesus (presumably), yet he confessed that the *Logos* was the Son of God. George Burns in his sacrilegious movie confessed that Jesus was the son of God, just as Mohammed and Buddha were. There were also some early professing Christians who held that Jesus is the Son of God by adoption. Does God dwell in such people and they in him?

Suppose next that someone confesses that Jesus is the Son of God, but does not repent? Luke 13:3 says, "Except ye repent, ye shall all likewise perish." Acts 17:30 says, God "now commandeth all men everywhere to repent." There was a prominent Presbyterian minister, strongly dispensational, who said he had never repented, that I had not either, and that no one in this age needs to. There are also enthusiastic evangelistic groups, most working on college campuses, that completely ignore repentance. The demon in Mark 1:24 said, "Let us alone . . . Jesus of Nazareth, . . . I know thee who thou art, the

Holy One of God." The demon did not use the word *Son,* but as "the Holy One of God" is its equivalent, the demon evidently recognized Jesus as the Son of God. Can we, on that basis, suppose that the demon was an angel of light? Is John therefore mistaken in saying that anyone who so confesses dwells in God and God in him? Suppose further that some people very consciously confess that Christ came in the flesh, is the Son of God, and that by his death he is the redeemer. They also insist on the virgin birth. But they do not believe that Christ's death was in itself sufficient to redeem us—necessary but not sufficient. So, in order to make up Christ's deficiencies, they not only do good works, but also have the supererogatory merits of the saints and martyrs transferred to their accounts. Is not this precisely the same sort of thing Paul so vehemently condemns in Galatians? The Judaizers wanted to supplement Christ's merits by observing the Mosaic food laws. And Peter fell into hypocrisy because of it.

It is clear, is it not, that the minimal, literal meaning of John's language can deceive us. We must seek a stricter, denotatively narrower, connotatively wider, meaning. Two words in the verse must be expanded. The first word is *confess.* Confession is a sincere public statement of a determinate religious commitment. That is to say, the demons knew and acknowledged that Jesus was the Son of God, but for them it was not a religious confession, but an admission begrudged by hate. The second word is *Son,* or *Son of God.* Demons no doubt have a very good idea of what this means, but George Burns did not have the foggiest. Similarly, most of the populace, including a large proportion of church members, are equally ignorant. What is needed is information. They must be brought to an understanding of the words. To be sure, after understanding the words, they may not confess; but they cannot confess without understanding.

This is clear, is it not? No, it is not. The understanding would include the creed of Chalcedon, the doctrine of the incarnation, already stressed by John, the meaning of propitiation eliminated by the NIV, and, and, how much else? Do all persons have to have the same extent of understanding? Very few devout Christians would expect a hill-billy to have and confess as much information as a seminary professor. The Scripture does not spell out such gradations, and maybe we are pleased to leave the determination to God's perfect judgment of one's sincerity and ability.

Nevertheless, we are obligated to organize congregations and admit members. For that matter, how can a denomination decide whom to ordain? A little before 1750 Gilbert Tennant decided that there were too many unconverted, unregenerate Presbyterian pastors in Pennsylvania, New Jersey, and New York. He made scathing accusations, some of which he was later forced to recant. Now, it seems true that during the eighteenth century, many of the English clergy lived scandalous lives. Their curates may have sincerely tried to encourage some Christian spirituality among the parishioners; but the rectors were essentially political appointees interested in the church only to the extent of receiving their salaries. The Scottish and Presbyterian criteria for ministers and members were orthodox theology (of course, the ministers were held to a higher academic standard), a life without public scandal, and regular participation in the Lord's Supper. The sessions and presbyteries disciplined, admonished, and sometimes expelled offenders. But this did not satisfy Gilbert Tennant. He insisted on a converted or regenerate ministry. And though he himself was disciplined for libel, the American Presbyterians since his day have tried to make some sort of "experience" one of their criteria.

This falls short of determining whether a candidate is regenerate or not. Naturally so, for no one can make such an infallible determination. The practice, if not the theory, remains very close to the old Scottish view, at least in those smaller Presbyterian denominations that still acknowledge and try to enforce the Westminster Standards. Communicant members are then received on a *credible* profession of faith. The session decides what is credible. And naturally, what is credible in the case of a poorly educated laborer is not or should not be credible if made by a Ph.D. in philosophy.

All this may seem unduly to complicate what appears to be a very simple verse. But these complications cannot be avoided if congregations are to have communicant members and ordained pastors.

4:16.   And we have known and have believed the love which God has in us. God is love, and he who dwells in love dwells in God and God dwells in him.

Some editors make a paragraph break in the middle of this verse. The second sentence could be a recapitulation, the new paragraph beginning with the next verse.

The first half of the verse presents a point of dispute, which, though it depasses the common limits of commentaries, may at least be stated for those who wish to go deeper into apologetics. The question relates to the relationship of faith to knowledge. One might hastily conclude from this verse that knowledge precedes belief or faith. The trouble is that in the Gospel 6:69 John has the same two verbs in the reverse order.

The solution carries us further than ordinary exegesis. That is to say, a great deal of Scripture must be examined and more than the usual number of inferences must be drawn. From Augustine to the present, Christian apologetes and philosophers have argued about the relation of faith to knowledge, of revelation to reason, of evidences to presuppositions. Most recently a book on apologetics has accused the present writer of abolishing all knowledge in favor of unsupported faith, while other apologetes accuse him of being a rationalist. To many theologians a man could not be guilty on both counts. What is necessary in a debate of this sort is a clear and precise definition of terms. Many people use both terms with no clear idea of what they are talking about. Secular writers also, uninterested in Christian faith, debate the nature of belief. The solution requires a full-fledged epistemology; and most Christian apologetes simply beg the question. They do not settle the question between intellectualism and voluntarism; and in their concentration on the authority of Scripture or the possibility of knowing God, they fail to test their theory with respect to mathematics and physics. Some say that some knowledge comes by revelation and other knowledge comes from sensation and observation. Some may also include innate or apriori knowledge. But in such a mixture, what has become of knowledge? What is the common quality and ultimate source of these three "knowledges"? A theory of knowledge, no matter what it is, must cover all items of knowledge. Restrict or expand the scope of possible knowledge as you wish, but let us avoid at all costs a resurrected form of the medieval theory of twofold truth.

Now, to return to the remainder of the verse: "We know and believe the love which God has in us." Presumably this refers to our belief in the incarnation and redemption as mentioned above in 4:9. Commentators who try to squeeze more out of this phrase fail to make their meaning clear.

The second half of the verse, in addition to repeating that God is love, goes on to assert that the man who dwells in God's love, dwells in God, and God dwells in him. These interwoven phrases with their reciprocal relationships stress the intimate fellowship between God and the believer. What is meant by intimate fellowship?

When I was a graduate student, there was a fellow student who came from an Irish family that had not long lived in America. Since there were an uncle and an aunt, plus children, there must have been at least two families. As they were somewhat isolated from their non-Irish neighbors, their family get-togethers were all the more intimate. I remember how my fellow student described the give and take, the wit and repartee as each one knew what the others were thinking. Even some non-Irish husbands and wives, if they do not follow the American custom of getting divorced every five years, can strangely know what the other is thinking before anything is spoken. This intimate fellowship consists of having the same ideas, of thinking alike, of being in extensive agreement. Hence, intimacy with God, too, consists in knowing what God thinks. That is to say, in knowing a good bit of theology.

This half-verse now becomes the basis for the next.

4:17.   By this is perfected the love with us that we may have confidence in the day of judgment because as he is so are we in this world.

The phrase, "By this" can only refer to the previous verse: By the fact of this intimate relationship, the indwelling of God in the believer and the believer in God, "the love with us is perfected." Attempts have been made to connect "By this" with "because as he is in us so we are in him." So far as grammar is concerned, the intervening phrase concerning confidence breaks the connection. Furthermore, it does not make good sense to say "Because he and we are both in the world, it follows that the love with us is perfected." It makes even less sense to say, "having confidence in the day of judgment is the cause of our deepening love." Our love is perfected now; the day of judgment is future. Therefore, the first interpretation above seems correct: By reason of mutual love, the love with us is perfected.

But could the verse mean, Because of our present confidence that

God will acquit us on the day of judgment, we are now perfecting our love? No, for the middle clause is either a purpose or result clause and does not tie in with the first two words, "By this."

Despite Lenski's refusal to take this clause as a purpose clause, the meaning rather clearly seems to be that our love, or God's love with us, is perfected *in order that,* or at the very least, with the result that, we may have confidence in the day of judgment. Lenski strangely insists that if we were to have confidence in the day of judgment, the verb should have been future. Thus, he arrives at the interpretation: our love is perfected, that is to say, we now have confidence respecting judgment day. But the conjunction *ina* should be taken as purposive (not epexegetical) whenever possible, and the verb is neither future nor present indicative. It is subjunctive, of which there is no future form. Hence, it is hard to understand the verse otherwise than: Because God remains in us, love is perfected, in order that. The idea is that we should no longer fear eternal punishment.

"The love *with* us" is a peculiar phrase. Does it mean God's love to us or our love to God? But the preposition is not *to;* it is *with.* Westcott notes that in Genesis 3:2 the text of the LXX has *with:* "the wife thou gavest *with* me." It is a very rare use of *meta.* Apparently then, unless someone can do better, the meaning is: the love of God to us is perfected by producing confidence in us respecting the day of judgment.

Lenski notes with reason that if we say our love to God gives us confidence, we shall have little confidence, for our love is always so imperfect that we are never sure we have a sufficient quantity or pure enough quality. How much does it take?

John's reference to the day of judgment requires notice also. Liberals charge that the disciples, disappointed that Christ did not return as he said he would, finally gave up that hope. But the later they date this Epistle and the Apocalypse, the less can they support their argument. John has already repeated the promise of Christ's return (3:2); here he makes a point of the judgment day. No, the eschatology of the apostles never changed. If anyone should try to eviscerate this meaning and refer it to any day of crisis (*kriseōs*) and martyrdom, the reply is that the context contains no such idea. There is fear of God in the next verse, but no fear of persecution.

The last phrase of the verse is, "because as he is, so also are we in this world." We might have expected "as Christ was, when he was in the world, unafraid, so are we now." Dare we then emphasize the present tense: As Christ now is, in his resurrection glory, so we, who remain in this world, are also? Well, "resurrection glory" makes it too strong. Obviously we do not now enjoy resurrection glory. Better is it to say, as Christ is now without fear, so we are without fear. This ties in well with the next verse: but note, it is not fear of persecution, but fear of God's punishment.

The present phrase began with the word *because*. Let us summarize the line of thought. The union of God and man in love brings God's love to fruition so that we may have confidence when we shall stand before his judgment seat because as Christ has no such fear, we also, being in him, have already lost all fear. The next verse supports this interpretation.

4:18. Fear does not exist in love, but perfect love expels fear because fear has [to do with] punishment, and he who fears is not perfected in love.

Love and fear are mutually exclusive. To my 14 pound Dachshund I probably looked like a giant. But I could jump up and make believe to pounce on him, and he would not fear, for he knew it was play and make believe. We loved each other. Then I later met a Doberman-pinscher, who growled at me as his hair stood up on the back of his neck. Doberman-pinschers have a bad reputation. But after I introduced myself to him according to the rules of canine etiquette, he led and accompanied me up and down the mountain. As a matter of fact, at the start, he virtually asked my permission to lead me. I did not fear him nor he me. Maybe we did not exactly love each other, for he was another man's dog; but we were very good friends.

This is a very low-level illustration for God's love to us; nevertheless, it shows how love expels fear. The illustration can be pushed one step further. A tiny Dachshund might have feared that I would beat him. I might have feared that the Doberman would bite me—indeed he could. Or, he might have feared me, had I picked up a fallen branch. But with love or friendship, he would expect me to throw the stick for him to retrieve. Fear has to do with punishment. And if one party or the other fears, he is not complete in his love.

This is still on a low level. Love of God, on the other hand, does not expel awe and reverence. I love dogs; some fine animal specimens I admire. Once I met a truly magnificent skunk, about three times the size of ordinary skunks, dignified and majestic. We looked each other over, I bowed to him, and each of us slowly moved off. But we do not admire God. We stand in awe, and reverence him. This may be called a godly fear; but it is not a cringing fear of punishment. That fear has been expelled.

4:19.   We love [him?] because he first loved us.

The *him* of the Textus Receptus is better omitted, not only because its manuscript evidence is weak, but also because the verse makes good sense, even better sense, without it. John has indeed been talking about God's love to us and our love to God. But he has also been talking about our love for fellow Christians. With the omission of the *him*, the phrase, the one word *agapōmen*, includes both love to God and love to Christians. The remainder of the short verse explains the reason for or source of this activity of loving; we love now because God first loved us. This love, of course, was the sacrifice of his Son.

There is a contrast in the Greek text that is missing in the usual translations. The pronoun *we* does not usually suggest emphasis, and even less the pronoun *he*. In Greek these subject pronouns are regularly omitted. But here they are both written out to form a decided contrast: We ourselves love, because he himself loved first.

4:20.   If anyone says, "I love God," and hates his brother, he is a liar. For he who does not love his brother whom he has seen, God whom he has not seen he cannot love.

One commentator says that "it is obviously easier to love and serve a visible man than an invisible God, and if we fail in the easier task, it is absurd to claim success in the harder." A. W. Pink denounces this view: "Nay, to put the matter on that footing is to degrade the grace of brotherly love, and wholly to destroy and overthrow the apostle's noble argument" (p. 190). He even continues on a human plane and points out that it is sometimes easier to love a man whom we have never seen than one whom we see daily.

The interpretation of the more recent commentator might have been acceptable if the text had said, *"how* can he love God whom he has not seen?"* The reading *how* is indeed attested by many cursives; *cannot* is attested by the combination of Aleph and B, plus a few cursives. This latter reading seems to make better sense. The question, "how can he love God" seems weak; whereas "he cannot" is a forceful assertion. The reason the question is weak is that it is far from obvious that it is easier to love and serve a visible man than an invisible God. Visible men, indeed visible Christian brothers, are often hard to love. It is much easier to sing the Doxology in church.

But if the text says "he cannot love God," we have an assertion that clears up the difficulty. If we love God—and not all who sing the Doxology in church do so—we obey his commandments, for love consists in fulfilling the law. The law specifies certain conduct toward Christian brethren. Then, and this time obviously, if we do not obey, we do not love either the Christian brother or the unseen God.

Much of the difficulty in this verse results from a misunderstanding of love. There are some people—actually, not fictionally or illustratively—who, impoverished by reckless and stupid financial conduct—demand, by an appeal to Scripture, that the minister share his meagre salary with them. Even after he has done so to the injury of his family, they keep demanding support as a matter of right, without amending their shiftlessness.

The same situation occurs on a much wider scale. Political programs for the relief of unemployment, and similar social legislation, receive support from some Christians who lack understanding of economics. Even if the bureaucrats were sincerely interested in helping the poor, instead of the corruption and kickbacks they solicit, it does not follow that a legislative program will be helpful just because it aims to be. British socialism has accomplished its aim of confiscating wealth, but it has made the poor poorer at the same time.

Such are the constant contemporary dangers in a misunderstanding of Christian love. They do not relieve us, however, of loving our brethren as God intended we should. What he intended us to do is spelled out in his law and precepts. We should obey them, doing neither less nor more.

4:21. And this commandment we have from him, that he who loves God should love his brother also.

Westcott holds that "from him" means "from the Father." He insists that the context requires it, since the Father only, and not Christ, is mentioned in verses 16-21. In spite of the context Stott wants the words to refer to Christ. The context should decide the issue, but for most people it makes no difference. Whether a commandment is given by the Father or by the Son, we are obliged to obey. The verse as a whole is a fitting summary conclusion for the last two-thirds of the chapter.

The Fifth Chapter

5:1. Everyone who believes that Jesus is the Christ has been begotten of God, and everyone who loves the begetter also loves him who is begotten of him.

THE outline we are following puts a break between verses two and three.

    B. Sonship Tested by Love   3:10b-23
    C. Sonship Tested by Belief   3:23-4:6
III. Closer Correlation of Righteousness, Love, and Belief   4:7-5:21
    A. Love and Belief   4:7-5:3
    B. Righteousness and Belief   5:3b-21

These divisions are probably the best. Yet we note that 5:1 introduces the theme of belief, without discontinuing the theme of love.

The first part of verse 1 is very important. For one thing it shows that faith is the result, not the cause, of regeneration: He who believes—present tense—has already been begotten—perfect tense. There is a theme in theology books called the *ordo salutis*. In plain Latin that means the order in which the stages of salvation follow one another. No evangelical would suspect that sanctification precedes justification, and it is impossibly stupid to suppose that glorification precedes regeneration. But does faith precede and cause regeneration? Some popular evangelists think so and urge people to stir up their natural abilities and believe in order to be regenerated. But obviously

a person dead in sin cannot believe. Faith is a gift of God, and it is the
first activity that God causes in the new life. This verse distinctly says
that everyone who believes has, already—perfect tense, been born
again. Unfortunately, many popular evangelists know very little
Scripture.

The desire to make regeneration the result of belief is coupled with
the notion that being born again is an *experience*. It is no more an
experience than being born the first time was. An adult convert may
almost immediately experience the result of regeneration, and even
recognize it as such; but the divine activity of resurrecting a man from
the dead and implanting in him a "habitus"—a scholastic term—
character, or nature, is not consciously perceived. We know it has
happened when we realize that we believe that Jesus is the Christ.

Even so, the verse can be misunderstood. What does it mean to say
that Jesus is the Christ? Only that that is what people now call him?
Scripture calls human kings, even King Saul, the Lord's Anointed.
The Apostle John must mean belief in what the Scriptures teach
about the Messiah. This was summarized in the Creed of Chalcedon.
How much of this creed, how much of the Scriptures, must we
understand and believe to be assured that we have been begotten of
God? It may be easier to know that we believe enough than that we
love or obey enough. At any rate we have the promise that he who
maintains Christ's doctrine shall never perish, ever.

For any adult of average intelligence belief in the propitiatory
efficacy of Christ's death is indispensable. This sacrifice causes us to
love him; and everyone who loves the begetter will also love those
who are begotten of him. John does not say that those who love God
ought to love the brethren. He states as a fact that they do. Love of the
brethren automatically follows regeneration. Therefore, by logical
contraposition one who does not love the brethren is not a Christian.

**5:2. By this we know that we love God's children, when
we love God and keep his commandments.**

The translation: It may make little difference to the sense, but the
verb *keep* is better attested than the verb *do* as given in the critical
editions. Metzger in his *Textual Commentary* acknowledges that the

phrase "do his commandments" is extremely rare, and that "keep his commandments" is "much more usual." Then he concludes that John must have written the unusual and could not have used the ordinary and regular expression. Must we believe that because John used "keep" in verse 3, he had to use "do" in verse 2?

The relationship between love and belief, which the context of this verse touches on, may further be clarified by a brief reference to other New Testament books. Paul teaches that we are justified by faith alone without works. Belief is the means of justification; and as an intellectual activity it is no more a basis of justification than love is. But love is a subsequent volitional activity. Though subsequent it is equally essential to full salvation. Let us construct an example. Belief in Christ does not exempt us from obedience to his commandments. We have no license to steal or commit adultery. Love to our wives as well as our duty toward God forbids adultery. Our resistance to temptation, if we are so tempted, not only shows our marital love to our wives, it also shows our Christian love to our neighbor's wife. Similarly, refraining from stealing our neighbor's property, and even helping him to earn more money if we can, is Christian love. But as we have already been justified, love can no more be the means of justification than it can be the basis. Obedience or love, as the result of belief, shows that our profession of faith is not hypocritical. To add a little emphasis to the words of James: If anyone *says* he has faith, but has no works, can that sort of faith save him?

5:3.   For this is what it means to love God, that we keep his commandments; and his commands are not oppressive.

The translation: The first phrase above is a paraphrase. Literally: For this is the love of God.

This commentary has emphasized its notion of love as obedience because of the very widespread contemporary notion that love is an emotion, and that emphasis on law is legalism. This deterioration within the relatively conservative churches is probably the result of the popularity of Freudian psychology. The earlier emphasis on volition has evaporated. Let the reader estimate the proportion of sermons on volition to those on emotion, and he will likely come up with a small fraction. Instead of a theocentric religion, egocentricity is common. Experience replaces Scripture and truth drowns in irrationality.

Now, God's intelligible commands may be difficult. No one keeps them perfectly. But they are not oppressive. Laxity and lawlessness give an initial impression of freedom. Heroin produces highs. But it results in hellish lows. The commands of God are for our good. His yoke is easy and his burden is light.

> **5:4.   . . . because everything begotten of God conquers the world; and this is the victory that conquers the world, our faith.**

The translation: *Conquer* and *victory* are the verb and noun forms of the same word. The word *conquest* might be used instead of *victory*, but the connotation is not quite right, and the emphatic repetition does not seem so strong as the Greek.

The interpretation of the preceding verse gave reasons why God's commandments are not oppressive. Here John condenses those reasons into half a sentence: because they conquer the world. It may seem strange that instead of saying "Everyone begotten of God," the text reads "everything," in the neuter. Many commentators, especially Lenski, simply take it as masculine. But Stott, following Plummer, gives a plausible explanation: "By the use of the neuter *whatsoever* John states the principle in its most general and abstract form. He does so to emphasize not 'the victorious *person*' but 'the victorious power.' "

It is true that this faith is our faith. We believe the message. But it is not our subjective cerebration that conquers the world: It is what we believe, namely, the faith. The next verse shows more of the personal element.

> **5:5.   Who [masculine] is he that conquers the world, if not he who believes that Jesus is the Son of God?**

In a sense each believer conquers the world to the extent that he resists worldly temptations. He recognizes that the Olympic games bestow a corruptible crown on those who waste their lives to win it; but our victory results in a crown of glory that fadeth not away. Nor is our struggle in most instances—in some, yes—a struggle against the pep drugs that modern athletes take. It is, however, an individual struggle. This fifth verse envisages the victory of individual Christians. This encouragement is important to the individual in question. But he should also be encouraged by the greater victory of verse 4. The individual Christian will conquer his temptations. Other individual Christians, theirs. With these contributions the faith will conquer the world.

The present evil world as a whole must be conquered. One individual Christian cannot do this. It is through the faith of many generations of Christians that a more complete victory will be attained. A postmillennarian could interpret this verse to mean that the gospel, in the course of ordinary preaching, will conquer the world until few or no heathen remain. The faith, the gospel, gains the victory. I do not believe that these verses can be pushed so far. The gospel may indeed conquer the world, but not necessarily through ordinary preaching alone; nor to the extent that every last individual will be saved. John has already referred to the second advent. True, these few references do not explain the details of eschatology. But if it be permissible to go beyond this Epistle and quote some phrases from the same author's Apocalypse (19:11-16), we read, "a white horse, and he that sat upon him was called Faithful and True [alēthinos] . . . his name is called the Word of God . . . and out of his mouth goeth a sharp sword, that with it he should smite the nations." The Word may be the gospel, proceeding from the rider's mouth: the gospel—good news for some, news of death for others. But it is a victory that no human preacher achieves.

However, to return to the Epistle, what needs more to be noted here is the combination of the believing Christian and what he believes. The last phrase of the verse is the message: Jesus is the Son of God.

In the Council of Nicaea Arius was willing to acknowledge Jesus as the Son of God and the first-begotten of all creation. Unlike Cerinthus, who held that Jesus was the natural son of Joseph and Mary, Arius had no objections to the virgin birth. For him Jesus was a superhuman being. One may even say that a virgin birth was necessary to Arius' theology. But he did not mean by "Son of God" what Athanasius meant. The doctrine of the Trinity asserts that the relation of the

Father to the Son is an eternal relation. The Father has always been Father because the Son has always been. But for Arius there was a time when there was no Son, and hence the Father has not always been Father. Therefore, it is not enough to confess in words that Jesus is the Son of God; we must confess the intellectual content of those words as expounded in Scripture. The reader of this commentary would do well to put it aside and immediately study the writings of Athanasius. Some theologians, whose Christianity is in doubt, assert that the doctrine of the Trinity, the doctrine of Athanasius, is seriously deformed by a large admixture of Greek philosophy. If the reader takes the good advice to turn immediately to Athanasius' *On the Decree,* he may be amazed at the amount of Scripture he uses, and the virtually complete absence of Greek philosophy—only one short reference in the whole book, if I remember correctly.

At this point the Aland text, following Westcott, makes a major paragraph break. Nestle did not. Stott and Bruce follow Aland. Lenski makes the break between verses 3 and 4. The outline followed in the present book seems better. The next verse describes in more detail who this Son of God is.

5:6.   This [Son] is he who came by water and blood, Jesus Christ; not by water only but by water and by blood; and the Spirit is the witness because the Spirit is the truth.

The text: In the first phrase some cursives substitute *spirit* for *blood.* Many more read: blood and spirit, or spirit and blood.

The translation: The last phrase can also be translated: the Spirit is Truth. Also, the last three instances of "by" can be translated "in."

Westcott suggests that the phrase "he that came" is an echo of "Blessed is he that cometh." Possibly. In any case John asserts an historical event 50 years prior—not a present encounter that cancels out two millennia.

But what is meant by water and blood? The reference to his coming might indicate the beginning of his ministry and hence the water might be his baptism. In which case, of course, the blood would be his death on the cross. Yet the mention of his death reminds us that in the Gospel 19:34 John records that when the spear pierced his side, "forthwith came there out blood and water." This interpretation, however, adopted by Pink, partially by Westcott, and others, is a product of romantic piety. In relation to the entire scene and significance of the death, this small detail hardly measures up to what the Epistle is saying. The baptism, with the descent of the Holy Spirit, much better announces his coming.

Much less can we allegorize water and blood to denote the sacraments of baptism and the Lord's Supper.

Another reason for interpreting the water as Jesus' baptism is the phrase, "not by water only but by water and by blood." This phrase cannot be intelligibly fitted into the other interpretations. What John had in mind was the view of some heretics who held that Jesus became the Son of God at his baptism, and that the Holy Spirit abandoned him on the cross before he died. John insists that though the baptism marks his public coming, he also came and accomplished his purpose by dying. The heretical view that only an ordinary man died altogether ruins the idea of a sacrificial satisfaction.

The final phrase of the verse is: The Spirit is the witness because the Spirit is truth. The word *witness* is a participle meaning "he who witnesses." In a court trial a certain man is called a witness. The witness gives his testimony. He swears to its truth. Here the Holy Spirit is the one who witnesses, and he does so because he himself is the truth. Remember that God is Truth; Jesus Christ is Wisdom, *Logos,* the Truth; the Spirit is the Spirit of Truth. That is what so irritates the irrational neoorthodox, who make truth an emotional encounter: *Wahrheit als Begegnung* (Emil Brunner). An infinitely irrational passion (Kierkegaard).

The idea that the Spirit witnesses to the truth puzzles some people. Romans 8:16 says that the Spirit himself witnesses (*summarturei,* witnesses *with,* not *to*) with our spirit. The Westminster Confession I, v says, "our full persuasion and assurance of the infallible truth [of the Bible] is from the work of the Holy Spirit, bearing witness by and with the Word in our hearts" (cf. also I, x).

Two points demand attention here. First, those of mystical tendencies find in such verses a basis for claiming to receive verbal communications from God. They assume the office of apostle. God speaks to them and thus they add to the canonical Scriptures. Such people may not explicitly claim to be apostles or add to the Scriptures; and the revelations they announce are not so often doctrinal as they are directions for solving either their own personal problems or those of their friends. Mr. Z has even gone so far as to insist that Mr. X should marry Miss Y, whom he hardly knows, because God told Mr. Z. These super devout mystics ought to test their divine receptivity on the stock market.

Then, second, liberal theologians object to biblical inerrancy on the ground (among others) that we do not know the "mode" of inspiration. Even some orthodox theologians are puzzled as to the mode of inspiration, though they willingly accept the result. It is hard to know what the latter are searching for, but easy to see what the former wish to evade. The mode of inspiration is simply that God puts his words into the prophets' mouths. The Old Testament repeats this idea many times; and Peter repeated it in Acts 4:25. To put it in more detail, God used the mental and literary abilities of each author in such a way that he wrote nothing but the truth. There is no mode or method: it is a direct exercise of omnipotence.[1]

The pious mystics and the lax liberals need to learn that the Spirit is Truth.

5:7. Because there are three witnesses.

The text: The Textus Receptus and the King James version contain several lines that are found in only one, and a very late, Greek manuscript. The words come from a fourth century Latin version. The story is that the Latin-reading ecclesiastics were incensed when Erasmus, in his first Greek edition, omitted the words in question. To defend himself Erasmus told them he would include the words if they could find a single Greek manuscript that had them. They quickly had a monk, so the story goes, write out a new manuscript in which he inserted his translation of the Latin into Greek. Compliant Erasmus thereupon inserted the words in his edition, and the King James version strangely kept them.

The recent effort to restore the authority of the so-called Byzantine

---

[1]See in tedious detail, *Predestination in the Old Testament,* now published together with *Biblical Predestination* as *Predestination,* 1987.

cursives as opposed to the uncials that the Christians for some reason did not see fit to reproduce, is not committed to the Textus Receptus in its entirety. The cursives do not support Erasmus' verse, and it will be omitted if a new edition based on the majority of manuscripts appears.

The translation: The first word is "Because." Most translations and many commentators, Lenski is an exception, substitute some other word.

To get on with the commentary, let us proceed immediately to the next verse, with a reference back to the preceding.

> **5:6, 7, 8.   . . . The Spirit is Truth because there are three witnesses, the Spirit, the water, and the blood, and these three are [in agreement] on the one [point].**

The word *because* fits nicely and is easily understood. In the Gospel, chapters 5 and 10, Jesus appeals to the Jewish legal principle that at least two witnesses are necessary to establish a truth. Here there are three. It does not weaken the argument that two of these three are not persons, but things. Hebrews 6:18 at least hints, and John 5:36 explicitly says that things can be witnesses. Thus the Spirit is Truth because there are three witnesses. These three bear witness that Jesus is the Son of God. The witnesses agree. We may recall that the false witnesses at Jesus' trial did not agree (Mark 14:56, 59).

> **5:9.   If we receive the witness of men, the witness of God is greater, because this is the witness of God [namely] that he has witnessed concerning his Son.**

A careless reader of the Bible is likely to pass over this verse with the vaguest of understanding. He will say to himself, "Well, of course, God is greater than man," without noting precisely what that witness was. It concerns Jesus as Son, clearly, but the time and place eludes notice. We ask, What was the witness and where was it given? F.F. Bruce gives the right answer, but passing over it in half a sentence goes on to irrelevancies. The witness occurred at Christ's baptism, when the voice from heaven said, "This is my beloved Son in whom I am

well pleased" (Matt. 3:17; cf. John 1:33). This is the correct interpretation because it fits the context; it fits the repeated mention of the water
in the preceding verses. One should not suppose, as Bruce seems to
suggest, that the apostle had his own witness in mind (John 20:31).
Nor Mark 15:39. This latter is the witness of a man, and as such could
be imagined to fit the verse in a negative sort of way, as contrasted with
the witness of God. But there is no hint that the apostle wishes to
specify negative instances. Furthermore, what the witness was is
unclear. The words could be translated, "This man was a son of a
god." But though the officer was a pagan Roman, he might have
meant more. He could have meant, "This man was a son of God," as
the NASB has it. The KJV and NIV translate it, "This man was the
Son of God." This is a perfectly possible translation, but one wonders
whether the centurion meant what we mean by the words. Or even
something resembling what we mean. It is true that the New Testament
presents Roman army officers in a good light. Yet there remains some
ambiguity. At any rate, and the less the centurion understood, the
witness of God is greater.

> **5:10.** **He who believes on the Son of God has the witness
> in himself; he who does not believe God makes him a liar
> because he has not believed in the witness which God has
> witnessed concerning his Son.**

The translation: The preposition after the words "He who believes"
is *eis*, in or to. After the following "not believe" there is a dative
without any preposition. "Believed" after the word *because* is *eis*
again, and the object is the witness or testimony. Those who wish to
defend special revelations to post-apostolic persons, and those who
try to distinguish between believing a message and believing a person,
on the basis of a preposition, versus no preposition, or the conjunction
that, will have great difficulty with this verse. *Eis* introduces first a
person and then a proposition; while the object *God* is a simple dative
without any prepositions. To believe a person is to believe what he
says. Strictly it is always the message, not the person, which is the
object of belief.

What then does John mean when he says we have the witness in
ourselves? Does it mean, "You ask me how I know he lives—he lives
within my heart"? This so-called gospel song was not written by a

neoorthodox author, but, unwittingly no doubt, reflects the neo-orthodox rejection of Scripture. Brunner, for example, believes in the resurrection not because of the biblical text; the Bible cannot be the ground of faith. he believes in the resurrection—however he defines it—by a faith that has nothing to do with history. To quote, "The Scripture is not the authority on the basis of which one believes in Christ" (*Die Christliche Lehre von Schöpfung und Erlösung*, p. 402). Bultmann says, "The believer therefore requires no testimony other than his own demonstrable witness" (p. 82).

Now, Arthur Pink was a very devout Christian. He had no tinge of neoorthodoxy as such. But, like others, he had a mystical tendency. To quote: "Literally, therefore, and in the strictest and fullest sense, I can have God's testimony in me . . . not of his Son offered and given to me . . . but of his Son . . . now dwelling in my heart. . . . This is something quite different from our own consciousness apprehending the truth and feeling the reality of what God testifies of his Son" (p. 212). This sort of language betrays a forgetfulness of what the witness is. The witness or testimony is, "This is my beloved Son in whom I am well pleased." This testimony is in us because, and in the sense that, we know and believe it. There is indeed a difference, a great difference between knowing or understanding the words of Matthew 3:17 and believing that God spoke them and that, therefore, they are true. There is no other way in which we can have a testimony in ourselves. Is this not what the verse very clearly says? "He who believes . . . [*ipso facto*] has the witness in himself." It is by means of this belief that we are justified, pardoned, acquitted, and accepted at God's bar of justice. The verse strongly emphasizes belief: "He who believes . . . he who does not believe . . . has not believed the testimony."

The negative part of the verse needs little explanation. He who does not believe what God says makes God a liar. Stong words, these; but incontrovertably true.

5:11, 12. **And this is the witness, that God has given us eternal life and this life is in his Son. He who has the Son has the life; he who does not have the Son of God does not have the life.**

These two verses may seem to be inconsistent with the interpretation here given of the preceding verses. At least they seem to refer to a testimony that goes beyond Matthew 3:17. Going beyond, however, does not mean excluding. The more extensive witness contains the first part, for Christ is the way, the truth, and the life—all three. Eternal life in the first instance means salvation from the pains of hell. Naturally, this life is in or by his Son, for it is by Jesus' death that we escape our just deserts. Of course, there is more to eternal life than this, but there could be no "more" without this. Eternal life includes our obedient love, our growth in grace, our resistance to temptation, our increasing holiness. These are all implicitly covered in the witness, "This is my beloved Son . . . *Hear ye him.*" The original witness at the baptism covers all that Jesus, and the apostles, later taught. None of the specifications just mentioned, however, nor their subsidiary divisions, would mean much apart from the justification that saves us from eternal death. Surely "this life is in his Son . . . he who does not have the Son does not have the life."

At this point in the Epistle there is a paragraph break. Though our outline tacks on the remainder to the last main heading, it would be equally satisfactory—that is to say, not quite satisfactory either way, to put 5:13-21 under a separate heading as "The Conclusion."

5:13.   These things I wrote to you in order that you might know that you have eternal life, you who believe on the name of the Son of God.

The word "these things" refers to the Epistle as a whole. Even if one wishes to restrict it to the first part of chapter 5, its material is so interwoven with many strands, that the whole Epistle is implicated.

The purpose of the Epistle is therefore to assure the readers of their eternal life. On this point Lenski is more clear than his Lutheran theology really allows. Nevertheless, he makes a mistake that many people share. To quote: "John uses *oida* as he does also in the three following notable statements (verses 18-20) and not *ginōskō*. His intention is not that he wants to exclude the knowing of the heart, which realizes with full effect upon the readers (*ginōskō*), but that he wants his readers to know also intellectually, with a clear understanding of the mind that they have life eternal only as believers. . . ."

Then Lenski emphasizes the need of this intellectual knowledge to combat Gnosticism or other heresies.

That this so-called intellectual knowledge is necessary for the purpose stated is something that needs emphasis. The rampant pietism of much professing evangelicalism is harmful to true Christianity. But the question Lenski should answer is, Is there any knowledge that is not intellectual? What does he mean by *ginōskō?* Lenski's distinction between *oida* and *ginōskō* is poor Greek and worse theology. A thorough word study of these verbs will not support any such sharp separation as Lenski supposes. In fact, the Old Testament, though written in Hebrew rather than Greek, makes the distinction impossible. In English Lenski's distinction is "the knowing of the heart" versus "a clear understanding of the mind." This is utterly unbiblical. It is almost true to say that Hebrew has no other term for *mind* than *heart.* It is the heart that thinks, either good thoughts or evil thoughts. Calculations of plans and consequences are activities of the heart. The reader may look up Psalm 12:2, 14:1, 15:2; Isaiah 6:10, 10:7, 33:18, 44:18–19, and a long list of similar verses. Whatever force contributing to the decadence of Protestantism the humanism external to the church has had, the internal source of its declension is anti-intellectualism. This was initiated by Schleiermacher, exacerbated by Kierkegaard, and popularized by neoorthodox existentialism. Only by a resuscitation of regard for truth can the present tendencies be reversed.

Assurance of eternal life can be deduced from a knowledge that one is a believer. Of course, as the negro spiritual says, "Everybody talking about heaven ain't goin there." With constant frequency people are assured of many things untrue. Indeed certainty increases in direct proportion to ignorance. The less educated a man is, the more things of which he is certain. If this obvious truth disturbs anyone, he should also realize that assurance is not essential to salvation. Different people have different mentalities. John Bunyan was so morbid he could hardly have had much assurance. With others more careless, doubts never arise. But if one knows, if one has a clear intellectual understanding that he believes, he should have legitimate assurance.

Enough has already been said concerning belief on the name of the Son of God. Again, let the reader read Athanasius.

5:14, 15.   And this is the boldness which we have toward him, that if we ask anything according to his will he hears us. And if we know that he hears us no matter what we ask, we know that we have the asked-for things which we have asked from him.

This is the same theme that troubled us at 3:22. Perhaps the difficulty appears here in an even more aggravated form. The difficulty is this: one interpretation makes the verse a falsehood. Indeed, if people want to reject scriptural inerrancy, they do better to stumble here than at the reign of Pekah or the size of a mustard seed. The other interpretation preserves inerrancy at the cost of making the verse tautological. Naturally, if God has willed that a certain event occur, and if then we pray for it, it will surely come to pass.

A. W. Pink, somewhat of an exception among commentators, makes an attempt to face the difficulty. In effect, his argument is that one need not know the will of God before making any request whatever. If one had to, it would be almost impossible to ask for anything. Petition would be prohibited. But Pink holds that there are exceptions. For example, Daniel knew by revelation that the captivity would end in its seventieth year. Therefore, his prayer for Israel's return was sure to be answered. But not only Daniel. Pink seems to think that some men, apart from revelation or infallibility, are "entitled on some extraordinary occasions to ask certain things to be done by God in his providence in the full assurance that they were according to his will" (p. 223). Whether there are such examples is a question. Pink acknowledges, however, that such unusual cases "can scarcely be held to meet the apostle's broad and general statement as to the efficacy of all believing prayer." He clearly does not want to reduce the verse to a tautology. His suggestion is, " 'If we ask anything according to his will'—may this not mean, 'If we ask anything as we believe that he wills it'?" But the following sentences, instead of giving instances, gradually move away from the problem, with the result that we cannot conclude that "according to his will" means "as we believe he wills it."

Verse 15 presents no additional difficulties; in fact, it is more obviously a tautology.

5:16, 17. If anyone see his brother sinning a sin not unto death, he shall ask, and he will give him life, to those who sin not to death. There is sin to death. I do not say that he should ask concerning it. All unrighteousness is sin, and there is a sin not to death.

The translation remains unpolished to preserve some of the original's style.

John's Gospel, for all its apparent simplicity, is profound; but it does not have the extremely puzzling difficulties, on less profound matters, that this Epistle has. In the Gospel many fail to see the implications; here many or nearly all fail to understand the premises.

The idea that a Christian brother can commit a sin unto death seems, first of all, to deny the doctrine of perseverance. Of course, the "brother" may be one in name only. Even so, it seems very strange that we should not pray for him. Christ refused to pray for the world, but we do not have his divine knowledge of who the reprobate are. We hope our brother is one of the elect, we even hope that some of the as-yet unconverted are elect, and so we pray for them. But can we know that Mr. X is reprobate, has committed the unpardonable sin, and so stop praying for him? This is not a profound point of doctrine like the Trinity or the atonement, but it seems to be more difficult.

The topic comes as a surprise. Nothing so far in the Epistle has prepared for it. It hardly fits the rubric of a conclusion. There is a verbal introduction, namely, the subject of prayer. Any logical connection is merely that this verse is one example of what to pray for and what not to pray for. But why *this* example is hard to say.

One commentator suggests that while it is right to pray for a brother who has sinned, maybe sometimes in our desire to save him from his sin we underevaluate the righteous claims of God. By forgetting God's holiness we virtually ask God to regard his sin excusable. The verse is supposed to warn against this. But surely this interpretation is farfetched.

In order to avoid deriving the Roman Catholic superstition of venial and mortal sins from this verse, the commentator continues by asserting that it is vain and presumptuous to identify any sin as a sin unto death. But in that case what can it mean to say, "If anyone see his brother sinning a sin not unto death"? To recognize that a sin is not unto death presupposes the recognition of its opposite; and this implication is enforced by the words, "There is a sin unto death. For this sin I do not say you should pray." Surely the two cases must be identified in order to distinguish between them.

John Cotton does better in identifying this sin. Indeed, he uses the argument of the immediately preceding words on this page, expressing it thus: "Some conceive that this sin is rarely found and difficult to discern; but then why does St. John write to common Christians not to pray for them? This is a sign they may be found and discerned" (p. 576). These two sentences form a sort of conclusion to his method of identification. Every sin is mortal, none venial, he says, because every sin deserves God's wrath and curse. But "there is a sin that not only in itself is deadly, but that irrevocably procures everlasting death (Matt. 12:31, 32; Mark 3:22)." Then Cotton gives the two distinguishing features of this sin. First, illumination of the mind. The sinner must have been illumined previously by the Spirit that the act in question is sin. "After this he sins willfully, there is no more hope of mercy." Second, there must be malice in the heart: it is done with spite and malice against the known truth (cf. Heb. 10:29). This sin is unpardonable.

All this sounds very much to the point. Neither Lenski nor Bruce is very helpful. Stott has some worthwhile observations; but Cotton is the best.

However, there remains another question: How can one man know that another sins with illumination and malice? The problem is not only to identify the characteristics of the sin, but to recognize those characteristics in an individual case. Note that my translation, following Westcott, does not say "a sin unto death," as if there were one definite deadly sin. The same sin in one man may be sin unto death, though in another it is not. The essential criteria are illumination and malice. Now the question becomes, How can we recognize these in another person?

Bruce attempts to limit our recognition to those cases where we see the physical death of the sinner, as in the case of Ananias and Sapphira. From this he concludes that John is prohibiting prayers for the dead. Parenthetically, for whatever conclusion the reader may wish to draw, it is not too clear that Ananias and Sapphira acted with malice.

Now Cotton, alone or almost alone, gives directions for detecting illumination and malice. If he fails to convince us of his criteria, at least he tries to do justice to the rather obvious fact that John thought it possible and even easy.

To quote:

> How may we discern when they commit this sin against the light and knowledge of the truth?
>
> If they express in their speech and conversation that they seek Christ and the ways of his grace, and say they are convinced that those ways are the right ways, and yet maliciously oppose those ways, then do not pray for them. The Pharisees knew Christ to be their heir, and yet tried to kill him (Matt. 2:38); and in the meantime they said he was a conjurer, and cast out devils through Beelzebub the prince of the devils; therefore Christ tells them their sins would never be forgiven them. (p. 579).

This does not quite tell us how to determine malice; but no commentator so far as I know has done better.

Now, there are one or two subsidiary matters. In describing the difficulties that were to be faced, and thus to stimulate serious attention, I mentioned a possible contradiction with the doctrine of perseverance. This is illusory. The text speaks of a brother sinning a sin not unto death. This is no statement that a brother can sin the unpardonable sin. The text says simply, "There is sin unto death." I suppose I tricked the reader a little bit by my wording in the paragraph on perseverance.

Then second, the death John has in mind, and the commentary proceeds on this assumption, is eternal death. Nothing in the Epistle supports the view that the death is physical.

Finally, and most insignificantly, with regard to the final phrase of verse 17, A. W. Pink wishes to omit the negative adverb. He will read it, 'There is a sin unto death.' This makes much better emphatic sense, but there is no manuscript evidence that supports it.

5:18.   We know that everyone begotten of God does not sin, but he who was begotten of God keeps himself, and the evil one does not touch him.

The notion of sinless perfection was refuted earlier. Here, too, the immediately preceding verses acknowledge that Christians sin. To repeat: perfectionism cannot use this Epistle to show that only some Christians achieve sinlessness. Those who talk about a second blessing, a victorious life, or perfect holiness, and carnal Christians, quite obviously allow that some Christians are not sinless. This admission prevents them from using this verse, for it says that all Christians enjoy whatever this verse is talking about. No Christian sins. The solution to the paradox is that the present tense indicates continuous action. No Christian continues in his previous sinful course. He continually makes progress in sanctification.

There is a pertinent negative example in John's Gospel, 9:31. When the Pharisees examined the man born blind, whose eyes Jesus had opened, the man said, "We know that God heareth not sinners." The blind man, though not a theologian, surely knew that all men sinned, including devout Jews: otherwise why should there have been a sacrificial system? The blind man knew that God had heard the prayers of Moses and David. Therefore, when he said, "God heareth not sinners," he was referring to habitual unrepentant sinners. Thus, in the Epistle, John is saying that truly repentant sinners do not continue their habitual sinning.

The next point does not appear so clearly in English; and in fact, it can be easily overlooked in Greek. The word born-again, or begotten, occurs in two forms. The first is *gegennēmenos*, and it obviously refers to any Christian. The second is *gennētheis*, introduced by the strong adversative *alla*, But! Careless reading might give the impression that the two forms refer to the same person—any ordinary Christian. But if the same person were meant, why the two forms?

This leads us to examine the object of the verb *touch*. There is considerable manuscript evidence to make this object *himself:* he who was born of God keeps himself so well that Satan cannot or at least does not touch him. But another group of manuscripts have *him, auton;* not *himself, eauton.*

These two considerations—the different verb form and the reading *auton*—combine to make the verse mean: Everyone begotten of God does not sin, but the begotten Son of God keeps him so that Satan cannot touch him.

There is a slight difficulty in this reading and interpretation, namely, the strong adversative *but.* One would expect *because* or at least *and.* Lenski prefers *himself* and has the two *begottens* refer to the same person. Yet the *but* presents the lesser difficulty.

5:19. We know that we are of God, and the whole world lies in the evil one.

The best commentary on this verse, or at least the second part of it, is the current newspapers.

5:20. We know that the Son of God has come, and has given us understanding that we might know the True One. And we are in the True One, in his Son Jesus Christ. This one is the true God and life eternal.

These three verses have each begun with an emphasis on knowledge. The object known in the last verse is the proposition that the Son of God has come. For a conclusion this is not at all inappropriate. Previous verses have emphasized the coming, the first coming, of the Messiah. He came by water and by blood. This we know. God has given us the intellectual ability (*dianoian*) to understand this. It is not an emotion or mystical experience, but an activity of understanding, intelligence, mind, as any lexicon will show. More exactly it is Christ who has given us the intelligence to know the true God. The text says, "The Son of God has come and has given us understanding." Yet the Son and the true God are not so sharply divided. The verse continues, we are in the True One, that is to say, we are in his Son Jesus Christ. To be in God and to be in Christ are the same thing. Even further, this one, Jesus Christ, is the true God. Jehovah's Witnesses make a lot—of nonsense—out of the absence of the article in John 1:1; but what can they do with this, article and all: Jesus Christ is the True God.

Some commentators, Stott, for example, weaken the sense of the word *true.* Intellect, truth, and understanding are not concepts always well received in this century. So they point out that the adjective here is, twice, *alēthinos,* not *alēthēs.* Stott says, "God is here described no as 'true,' *alēthēs,* but as 'real' (NEB), *alēthinos.*

Anyone who knows the Greek alphabet can look up the two adjec tives in Liddell and Scott, Volume I, page 64. For *alēthēs* they have "*unconcealed,* so *true, real,* opp. *false, apparent* . . . of persons, *truthful, honest* . . . of oracles, *true, unerring.*" For *alēthinos* they have, "of persons, *truthful, trusty* . . . of things, *true, genuine.*" For those who are willing to go to a little more trouble, Hermas, *Mandate* 3:1 says, "*o kurios alēthinos en panti rhemati.*" This cannot mean "the real Lord." It has to mean "The Lord is truthful in every word." Therefore, the attempt to banish truth from the adjective *alēthinos* fails. Both in the Gospel and in the Epistle John is strong on truth.

Of course, *alēthinos* can sometimes be translated "real"; but so can *alēthēs.* It is hard to find any difference in meaning between the two adjectives. Here the repetition of knowing, three times, and the word *understanding,* and the proposition "the Son of God has come," all favor the idea of truth.

5:21. Children, guard yourselves against idols.

This is not such an abrupt and disconnected conclusion as it at first appears. We are likely to think of the silver images of Artemis in Ephesus, or the wayside statues in Achaia. But nothing in the Epistle prepares for this. The idols John has in mind are the heretical doctrines of Cerinthus or other false teachers. The emphasis is still on truth. The enemy is false teaching, inspired by the evil one. Let the truth prevail—today, also.

Scripture Index

Index

The Crisis of Our Time

Historians have christened the thirteenth century the Age of Faith and termed the eighteenth century the Age of Reason. The twentieth century has been called many things: the Atomic Age, the Age of Inflation, the Age of the Tyrant, the Age of Aquarius. But it deserves one name more than the others: the Age of Irrationalism. Contemporary secular intellectuals are anti-intellectual. Contemporary philosophers are anti-philosophy. Contemporary theologians are anti-theology.

In past centuries secular philosophers have generally believed that knowledge is possible to man. Consequently they expended a great deal of thought and effort trying to justify knowledge. In the twentieth century, however, the optimism of the secular philosophers has all but disappeared. They despair of knowledge.

Like their secular counterparts, the great theologians and doctors of the church taught that knowledge is possible to man. Yet the theologians of the twentieth century have repudiated that belief. They also despair of knowledge. This radical skepticism has filtered down from the philosophers and theologians and penetrated our entire culture, from television to music to literature. *The Christian in the twentieth century is confronted with an overwhelming cultural consensus—sometimes stated explicitly, but most often implicitly: Man does not and cannot know anything truly.*

What does this have to do with Christianity? Simply this: If man can know nothing truly, man can truly know nothing. We cannot know that the Bible is the Word of God, that Christ died

for the sins of his people, or that Christ is alive today at the right
hand of the Father. Unless knowledge is possible, Christianity is
nonsensical, for it claims to be knowledge. What is at stake in the
twentieth century is not simply a single doctrine, such as the
Virgin Birth, or the existence of hell, as important as those
doctrines may be, but the whole of Christianity itself. If knowledge is not possible to man, it is worse than silly to argue points
of doctrine—it is insane.

The irrationalism of the present age is so thorough-going
and pervasive that even the Remnant—the segment of the
professing church that remains faithful—has accepted much of
it, frequently without even being aware of what it was accepting.
In some circles this irrationalism has become synonymous with
piety and humility, and those who oppose it are denounced as
rationalists—as though to be logical were a sin. Our contemporary anti-theologians make a contradiction and call it a Mystery.
The faithful ask for truth and are given Paradox. If any balk at
swallowing the absurdities of the anti-theologians, they are
frequently marked as heretics or schismatics who seek to act
independently of God.

There is no greater threat facing the true Church of Christ at
this moment than the irrationalism that now controls our entire
culture. Totalitarianism, guilty of tens of millions of murders,
including those of millions of Christians, is to be feared, but not
nearly so much as the idea that we do not and cannot know the
truth. Hedonism, the popular philosophy of America, is not to be
feared so much as the belief that logic— that "mere human
logic," to use the religious irrationalists' own phrase—is futile.
The attacks on truth, on revelation, on the intellect, and on logic
are renewed daily. But note well: The misologists—the haters of
logic—use logic to demonstrate the futility of using logic. The
anti-intellectuals construct intricate intellectual arguments to
prove the insufficiency of the intellect. The anti-theologians use
the revealed Word of God to show that there can be no revealed
Word of God—or that if there could, it would remain impene-
trable darkness and Mystery to our finite minds.

Nonsense Has Come

Is it any wonder that the world is grasping at straws—the

straws of experientialism, mysticism and drugs? After all, if people are told that the Bible contains insoluble mysteries, then is not a flight into mysticism to be expected? On what grounds can it be condemned? Certainly not on logical grounds or Biblical grounds, if logic is futile and the Bible unintelligible. Moreover, if it cannot be condemned on logical or Biblical grounds, it cannot be condemned at all. If people are going to have a religion of the mysterious, they will not adopt Christianity: They will have a genuine mystery religion. "Those who call for Nonsense," C.S. Lewis once wrote, "will find that it comes." And that is precisely what has happened. The popularity of Eastern mysticism, of drugs, and of religious experience is the logical consequence of the irrationalism of the twentieth century. There can and will be no Christian revival—and no reconstruction of society—unless and until the irrationalism of the age is totally repudiated by Christians.

The Church Defenseless

Yet how shall they do it? The spokesmen for Christianity have been fatally infected with irrationalism. The seminaries, which annually train thousands of men to teach millions of Christians, are the finishing schools of irrationalism, completing the job begun by the government schools and colleges. Some of the pulpits of the most conservative churches (we are not speaking of the apostate churches) are occupied by graduates of the anti-theological schools. These products of modern anti-theological education, when asked to give a reason for the hope that is in them, can generally respond with only the intellectual analogue of a shrug—a mumble about Mystery. They have not grasped—and therefore cannot teach those for whom they are responsible—the first truth: "And ye shall know the truth." Many, in fact, explicitly deny it, saying that, at best, we possess only "pointers" to the truth, or something "similar" to the truth, a mere analogy. Is the impotence of the Christian Church a puzzle? Is the fascination with pentecostalism and faith healing among members of conservative churches an enigma? Not when one understands the sort of studied nonsense that is purveyed in the name of God in the seminaries.

The Trinity Foundation

The creators of The Trinity Foundation firmly believe that theology is too important to be left to the licensed theologians —the graduates of the schools of theology. They have created The Trinity Foundation for the express purpose of teaching the faithful all that the Scriptures contain—not warmed over, baptized, secular philosophies. Each member of the board of directors of The Trinity Foundation has signed this oath: "I believe that the Bible alone and the Bible in its entirety is the Word of God and, therefore, inerrant in the autographs. I believe that the system of truth presented in the Bible is best summarized in the Westminster Confession of Faith. So help me God."

The ministry of The Trinity Foundation is the presentation of the system of truth taught in Scripture as clearly and as completely as possible. We do not regard obscurity as a virtue, nor confusion as a sign of spirituality. Confusion, like all error, is sin, and teaching that confusion is all that Christians can hope for is doubly sin.

The presentation of the truth of Scripture necessarily involves the rejection of error. The Foundation has exposed and will continue to expose the irrationalism of the twentieth century, whether its current spokesman be an existentialist philosopher or a professed Reformed theologian. We oppose anti-intellectualism, whether it be espoused by a neo-orthodox theologian or a fundamentalist evangelist. We reject misology, whether it be on the lips of a neo-evangelical or those of a Roman Catholic charismatic. To each error we bring the brilliant light of Scripture, proving all things, and holding fast to that which is true.

The Primacy of Theory

The ministry of The Trinity Foundation is not a "practical" ministry. If you are a pastor, we will not enlighten you on how to organize an ecumenical prayer meeting in your community or how to double church attendance in a year. If you are a homemaker, you will have to read elsewhere to find out how to become a total woman. If you are a businessman, we will not tell you how to develop a social conscience. The professing church is drowning in such "practical" advice.

The Trinity Foundation is unapologetically theoretical in its outlook, believing that theory without practice is dead, and that practice without theory is blind. The trouble with the professing church is not primarily in its practice, but in its theory. Christians do not know, and many do not even care to know, the doctrines of Scripture. Doctrine is intellectual, and Christians are generally anti-intellectual. Doctrine is ivory tower philosophy, and they scorn ivory towers. The ivory tower, however, is the control tower of a civilization. It is a fundamental, theoretical mistake of the practical men to think that they can be merely practical, for practice is always the practice of some theory. The relationship between theory and practice is the relationship between cause and effect. If a person believes correct theory, his practice will tend to be correct. The practice of contemporary Christians is immoral because it is the practice of false theories. It is a major theoretical mistake of the practical men to think that they can ignore the ivory towers of the philosophers and theologians as irrelevant to their lives. Every action that the "practical" men take is governed by the thinking that has occurred in some ivory tower—whether that tower be the British Museum, the Academy, a home in Basel, Switzerland, or a tent in Israel.

In Understanding Be Men

It is the first duty of the Christian to understand correct theory—correct doctrine—and thereby implement correct practice. This order—first theory, then practice—is both logical and Biblical. It is, for example, exhibited in Paul's epistle to the Romans, in which he spends the first eleven chapters expounding theory and the last five discussing practice. The contemporary teachers of Christians have not only reversed the order, they have inverted the Pauline emphasis on theory and practice. The virtually complete failure of the teachers of the professing church to instruct the faithful in correct doctrine is the cause of the misconduct and cultural impotence of Christians. The Church's lack of power is the result of its lack of truth. The *Gospel* is the power of God, not religious experience or personal relationship.

The Church has no power because it has abandoned the Gospel, the good news, for a religion of experientialism. Twentieth century American Christians are children carried about by every wind of doctrine, not knowing what they believe, or even if they believe anything for certain.

The chief purpose of The Trinity Foundation is to counteract the irrationalism of the age and to expose the errors of the teachers of the church. Our emphasis—on the Bible as the sole source of truth, on the primacy of the intellect, on the supreme importance of correct doctrine, and on the necessity for systematic and logical thinking—is almost unique in Christendom. To the extent that the church survives—and she will survive and flourish—it will be because of her increasing acceptance of these basic ideas and their logical implications.

We believe that the Trinity Foundation is filling a vacuum in Christendom. We are saying that Christianity is intellectually defensible—that, in fact, it is the only intellectually defensible system of thought. We are saying that God has made the wisdom of this world—whether that wisdom be called science, religion, philosophy, or common sense—foolishness. We are appealing to all Christians who have not conceded defeat in the intellectual battle with the world to join us in our efforts to raise a standard to which all men of sound mind can repair.

The love of truth, of God's Word, has all but disappeared in our time. We are committed to and pray for a great instauration. But though we may not see this reformation of Christendom in our lifetimes, we believe it is our duty to present the whole counsel of God because Christ has commanded it. The results of our teaching are in God's hands, not ours. Whatever those results, his Word is never taught in vain, but always accomplishes the result that he intended it to accomplish. Professor Gordon H. Clark has stated our view well:

There have been times in the history of God's people, for example, in the days of Jeremiah, when refreshing grace and widespread revival were not to be expected: the time was one of chastisement. If this twentieth century is of a similar nature, individual Christians here and there can find comfort and strength in a study of God's Word. But if God has decreed happier days for us and if we may expect a world-shaking and genuine spiritual awakening, then it is the author's belief that a zeal for souls, however necessary, is not the sufficient condition. Have there not been devout saints in every age, numerous enough to carry on a revival? Twelve such persons are plenty. What distinguishes the arid ages from the period of the Reformation, when nations were moved as they had not been since Paul preached in Ephesus, Corinth, and Rome, is the latter's fullness of knowledge of God's Word. To echo an early Reformation thought, when the ploughman and the garage attendant know the Bible as well as the theologian does, and know it better than some contemporary theologians, then the desired awakening shall have already occurred.

In addition to publishing books, of which *First John: A Commentary* is the second, the Foundation publishes a bimonthly newsletter, *The Trinity Review*. Subscriptions to *The Review* are free; please write to the address below to become a subscriber. If you would like further information or would like to join us in our work, please let us know.

The Trinity Foundation is a non-profit foundation tax-exempt under section 501 (c)(3) of the Internal Revenue Code of 1954. You can help us disseminate the Word of God through your tax-deductible contributions to the Foundation.

And we know that the Son of God is come, and hath given us an understanding, that we may know him that is true, and we are in him that is true, in his Son Jesus Christ. This is the true God, and eternal life.

John W. Robbins

Intellectual
Ammunition

The Trinity Foundation is committed to the reconstruction of philosophy and theology along Biblical lines. We regard God's command to bring all our thoughts into conformity with Christ very seriously, and the books listed below are designed to accomplish that goal. They are written with two subordinate purposes: (1) to demolish all secular claims to knowledge; and (2) to build a system of truth based upon the Bible alone.

Philosophy

Behaviorism and Christianity, Gordon H. Clark $6.95

Behaviorism is a critique of both secular and religious behaviorists. It includes chapters on John Watson, Edgar S. Singer Jr., Gilbert Ryle, B.F. Skinner, and Donald MacKay. Clark's refutation of behaviorism and his argument for a Christian doctrine of man are unanswerable.

A Christian Philosophy of Education, Gordon H. Clark $8.95

The first edition of this book was published in 1946. It sparked the contemporary interest in Christian schools. Dr. Clark has thoroughly revised and updated it, and it is needed now more than ever. Its chapters include: The Need for a World-View, The Christian World-View, The Alternative to Christian Theism, Neutrality, Ethics, The Christian Philosophy of Education, Academic Matters, Kindergarten to University. Three appendices are included as well: The Relationship of Public Education to Christianity, A Protestant World-View, and Art and the Gospel.

A Christian View of Men and Things, Gordon H. Clark $10.95
   No other book achieves what A Christian View *does: the presentation of Christianity as it applies to history, politics, ethics, science, religion, and epistemology. Clark's command of both worldly philosophy and Scripture is evident on every page, and the result is a breathtaking and invigorating challenge to the wisdom of this world.*

Clark Speaks From The Grave, Gordon H. Clark $3.95
   Dr. Clark chides some of his critics for their failure to defend Christianity competently. Clark Speaks *is a stimulating and illuminating discussion of the errors of contemporary apologists.*

Education, Christianity, and the State $7.95
J. Gresham Machen
   Machen was one of the foremost educators, theologians, and defenders of Christianity in the twentieth century. The author of numerous scholarly books, Machen saw clearly that if Christianity is to survive and flourish, a system of Christian grade schools must be established. This collection of essays captures his thought on education over nearly three decades.

Essays on Ethics and Politics $10.95
Gordon H. Clark
   Clark's s essays, written over the course of five decades, are a major statement of Christian ethics.

Gordon H. Clark: Personal Recollections $6.95
John W. Robbins, editor
   Friends of Dr. Clark have written their recollections of the man. Contributors include family members, colleagues, students, and friends such as Harold Lindsell, Carl Henry, Ronald Nash, Dwight Zeller, and Mary Crumpacker. The book includes an extensive bibliography of Clark's work.

John Dewey, Gordon H. Clark $2.00
   America has not produced many philosophers, but John Dewey has been extremely influential. Clark examines his philosophy of Instrumentalism.

Logic, Gordon H. Clark $8.95
Written as a textbook for Christian schools, Logic *is another unique book from Clark's pen. His presentation of the laws of thought, which must be followed if Scripture is to be understood correctly, and which are found in Scripture itself, is both clear and thorough.* Logic *is an indispensable book for the thinking Christian.*

The Philosophy of Science and Belief in God $5.95
Gordon H. Clark
In opposing the contemporary idolatry of science, Clark analyzes three major aspects of science: the problem of motion, Newtonian science, and modern theories of physics. His conclusion is that science, while it may be useful, is always false; and he demonstrates its falsity in numerous ways. Since science is always false, it can offer no objection to the Bible and Christianity.

Religion, Reason and Revelation, Gordon H. Clark $7.95
One of Clark's apologetical masterpieces, Religion, Reason and Revelation *has been praised for the clarity of its thought and language. It includes chapters on Is Christianity a Religion? Faith and Reason, Inspiration and Language, Revelation and Morality, and God and Evil. It is must reading for all serious Christians.*

Thales to Dewey: A History of Philosophy   paper $11.95
Gordon H. Clark   hardback $16.95
This volume is the best one volume history of philosophy in English.

Three Types of Religious Philosophy, Gordon H. Clark $6.95
In this book on apologetics, Clark examines empiricism, rationalism, dogmatism, and contemporary irrationalism, which does not rise to the level of philosophy. He offers a solution to the question, "How can Christianity be defended before the world?"

Theology

The Atonement, Gordon H. Clark $8.95

This is a major addition to Clark's multi-volume systematic theology. In The Atonement, *Clark discusses the Covenants, the Virgin Birth and Incarnation, federal headship and representation, the relationship between God's sovereignty and justice, and much more. He analyzes traditional views of the Atonement and criticizes them in the light of Scripture alone.*

The Biblical Doctrine of Man, Gordon H. Clark $6.95

Is man soul and body or soul, spirit, and body? What is the image of God? Is Adam's sin imputed to his children? Is evolution true? Are men totally depraved? What is the heart? These are some of the questions discussed and answered from Scripture in this book.

Cornelius Van Til: The Man and The Myth $2.45
John W. Robbins

The actual teachings of this eminent Philadelphia theologian have been obscured by the myths that surround him. This book penetrates those myths and criticizes Van Til's surprisingly unorthodox views of God and the Bible.

Faith and Saving Faith, Gordon H. Clark $6.95

The views of the Roman Catholic church, John Calvin, Thomas Manton, John Owen, Charles Hodge, and B.B. Warfield are discussed in this book. Is the object of faith a person or a proposition? Is faith more than belief? Is belief more than thinking with assent, as Augustine said? In a world chaotic with differing views of faith, Clark clearly explains the Biblical view of faith and saving faith.

God's Hammer: The Bible and Its Critics $6.95
Gordon H. Clark

The starting point of Christianity, the doctrine on which all other doctrines depend, is "The Bible alone is the Word of God written, and therefore inerrant in the autographs." Over the centuries the opponents of Christianity, with Satanic shrewdness,

have concentrated their attacks on the truthfulness and complete-
ness of the Bible. In the twentieth century the attack is not so much
in the fields of history and archaeology as in philosophy. Clark's
brilliant defense of the complete truthfulness of the Bible is
captured in this collection of eleven major essays.

Guide to the Westminster Confession and Catechism $13.95
James E. Bordwine
    This large book contains the full text of both the Westminster
Confession (both original and American versions) and the Larger
Catechism. In addition, it offers a chapter-by-chapter summary of
the Confession and a unique index to both the Confession and the
Catechism.

The Incarnation, Gordon H. Clark $8.95
    Who was Christ? The attack on the Incarnation in the
nineteenth and twentieth centuries has been vigorous, but the
orthodox response has been lame. Clark reconstructs the doctrine
of the Incarnation building and improving upon the Chalcedonian
definition.

In Defense of Theology, Gordon H. Clark $9.95
    There are four groups to whom Clark addresses this book: the
average Christians who are uninterested in theology, the atheists
and agnostics, the religious experientialists, and the serious
Christians. The vindication of the knowledge of God against the
objections of three of these groups is the first step in theology.

The Johannine Logos, Gordon H. Clark $5.95
    Clark analyzes the relationship between Christ, who is the
truth, and the Bible. He explains why John used the same word to
refer to both Christ and his teaching. Chapters deal with the
Prologue to John's Gospel, Logos and Rheemata, Truth, and
Saving Faith.

Logical Criticisms of Textual Criticism $3.25
Gordon H. Clark
    In this critique of the science of textual criticism, Dr. Clark
exposes the fallacious argumentation of the modern textual critics
and defends the view that the early Christians knew better than the

modern critics which manuscripts of the New Testament were more accurate.

Pat Robertson: A Warning to America, John W. Robbins $6.95
The Protestant Reformation was based on the Biblical principle that the Bible is the only revelation from God, yet a growing religious movement, led by Pat Robertson, asserts that God speaks to them directly. This book addresses the serious issue of religious fanaticism in America by examining the theological views of Pat Robertson.

Predestination, Gordon H. Clark $8.95
Clark thoroughly discusses one of the most controversial and pervasive doctrines of the Bible: that God is, quite literally, Almighty. Free will, the origin of evil, God's omniscience, creation, and the new birth are all presented within a Scriptural framework. The objections of those who do not believe in the Almighty God are considered and refuted. This edition also contains the text of the booklet, Predestination in the Old Testament.

Scripture Twisting in the Seminaries. Part 1: Feminism $5.95
John W. Robbins
An analysis of the views of three graduates of Westminster Seminary on the role of women in the church.

Today's Evangelism: Counterfeit or Genuine? $6.95
Gordon H. Clark
Clark compares the methods and messages of today's evangelists with Scripture, and finds that Christianity is on the wane because the Gospel has been distorted or lost. This is an extremely useful and enlightening book.

The Trinity, Gordon H. Clark $8.95
Apart from the doctrine of Scripture, no teaching of the Bible is more important than the doctrine of God. Clark's defense of the orthodox doctrine of the Trinity is a principal portion of a major new work of Systematic Theology now in progress. There are chapters on the deity of Christ, Augustine, the incomprehensibility of God, Bavinck and Van Til, and the Holy Spirit, among others.

What Do Presbyterians Believe? Gordon H. Clark $7.95
   This classic introduction to Christian doctrine has been republished. It is the best commentary on the Westminster Confession of Faith that has ever been written.

Commentaries on the New Testament

Colossians, Gordon H. Clark $6.95
Ephesians, Gordon H. Clark $8.95
First Corinthians, Gordon H. Clark $10.95
First John, Gordon H. Clark $10.95
First and Second Thessalonians, Gordon H. Clark $5.95
The Pastoral Epistles (I and II Timothy and Titus) $9.95
   Gordon H. Clark
   All of Clark's commentaries are expository, not technical, and are written for the Christian layman. His purpose is to explain the text clearly and accurately so that the Word of God will be thoroughly known by every Christian.

The Trinity Library

We will send you one copy of each of the 35 books listed above for the low price of $175. The regular price of these books is $270. You may also order the books you want individually on the order blank on the next page. Because some of the books are in short supply, we must reserve the right to substitute others of equal or greater value in The Trinity Library. This special offer expires June 30, 1994.

Order Form

Name _____

Address _____

_____

Please: ☐ add my name to the mailing list for *The Trinity Review*. I understand that there is no charge for the *Review*.

         ☐ accept my tax deductible contribution of $_____ for the work of the Foundation.

         ☐ send me _____ copies of *First John: A Commentary*. I enclose as payment $ _____.

         ☐ send me the Trinity Library of 35 books. I enclose $175 as full payment for it.

         ☐ send me the following books. I enclose full payment in the amount of $ _____ for them.

_____

_____

_____

_____

_____

_____

_____

Mail to: The Trinity Foundation
Post Office Box 700
Jefferson, MD 21755

Please add $2.50 for postage on orders less than $10. Thank you.
For quantity discounts, please write to the Foundation.